War and Cinema

V

War and Cinema

The Logistics of Perception

———————◆———————

PAUL VIRILIO

Translated by Patrick Camiller

VERSO

London · New York

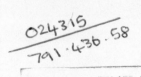
Photograph of author on back cover by G. Crossay.

First published by Cahiers du cinéma/Editions de l'Etoile 1984
This edition published by Verso 1989
Reprinted 1992
© Paul Virilio 1984
© This translation, Verso 1989

Verso
UK: 6 Meard Street, London W1V 3HR
USA: 29 West 35th Street, New York, NY 10001-2291

Verso is the imprint of New Left Books

British Library Cataloguing in Publication Data
Virilio, Paul, 1932–
    War and cinema: the logistics of perception.
    1. Cinema films. Special subjects: Warfare
    I. Title
    791.43'09'09358

    ISBN 0-86091-214-0
    ISBN 0-86091-928-5 pbk

US Library of Congress Cataloging in Publication Data
Virilio, Paul.
    [Guerre et cinéma. English]
    War and cinema: the logistics of perception/Paul Virilio;
translated by Patrick Camiller.
        p. cm.
    Translation of: Guerre et cinéma.
    Includes bibliographical references.
    ISBN 0-86091-214-0: —ISBN 0-86091-928-5 (pbk,):
    1. War films—History and criticism.   I. Title.
PN1995.9.W3V58   1989
791.43'09'09358—dc19

Typeset by Leaper & Gard Ltd, Bristol, England
Printed in Great Britain by Dotesios Ltd, Trowbridge, Wiltshire

Contents

Acknowledgements

Acknowledgements are due to the following people and institutions for permission to reproduce photographs used as illustrations:

La Recherche, Paris 1983: *1*. Imperial War Museum, London: *2, 3, 7*. Col Roy M. Stanley, *Photo Intelligence*, Sidgwick and Jackson, London 1982: *5, 6, 12, 16, 26, 27, 28, 29, 30, 31, 32, 33, 34, 35, 36, 37, 38, 39, 40, 41*. *Nueva Forma*, Madrid 1973: *14*. *L'Histoire en image*, Cercle Européen du Livre: *17*. E. Steichen, *American Aerial Photography at the Front*, US Air Service 1919: *8*. *Signal* 1941: *18*. *After the Battle* no. 41, 1983: *42, 44*. C. Bowyer, *Pathfinders at War*, Ian Allan, London 1977: *23, 24, 25*. Mallory and Ottar, *Architecture of Aggression*, Architectural Press, London 1973: *19, 20, 22*. David Shermer, *The Great War*, Octopus, London 1973: *4, 9*. 'Cine MBXA', *Ciné Doc*, Paris 1983: *11*. R. Chambe, *Histoire de l'aviation*, Flammarion, Paris 1972: *15*. *Cosmos Encyclopédie* no. 2, 1970: *47*. *Daidalos* no. 3: *43*. N. Frankland, *Bomber Offensive*, Purnell's, London 1969: *21*. *Culture Technique* no. 10, 1983: *13, 45*.

War is the art of embellishing death.
  Japanese maxim

Preface to the English Edition: The Sight Machine

This essay investigates the systematic use of cinema techniques in the conflicts of the twentieth century. It is an approach that has never been adopted before, or hardly ever. Yet the strategic and tactical necessities of cartography were known long ago, and in the line from the emergence of military photography in the American Civil War to today's video surveillance of the battlefield, the intensive use of film sequences in aerial reconnaissance was already developing during the First World War. The general staffs had no other means of regularly updating their picture of reality, as artillery constantly turned the terrain upside down and removed the topographical references crucial to the organization of battle.

On board an aeroplane, the camera's peep-hole served as an indirect sighting device complementing those attached to the weapons of mass destruction. It thus prefigured a symptomatic shift in target-location and a growing derealization of military engagement. For in industrialized warfare, where the representation of events outstripped the presentation of facts, the image was starting to gain sway over the object, time over space. Soon a conflict of strategic and political interpretation would ensue, with radio and then radar completing the picture.

As it laid the ground for a veritable *logistics of military perception*, in which a supply of images would become the equivalent of an ammunition supply, the 1914–18 war compounded a new 'weapons system' out of combat vehicle and camera – a kind of advanced cinema dolly, one might say. After the Second World War, it became possible to sketch out a strategy of *global vision*, thanks to spy-satellites, drones and other video-missiles, and above all to the appearance of a new type of headquarters. The central electronic-warfare administration – such as the so-called '3Ci' (control, command, communication, intelligence) in place in each major

1

power – can now attend in real time to the images and data of a planetary conflict. Thus, alongside the army's traditional 'film department' responsible for directing propaganda to the civilian population, a military 'images department' has sprung up to take charge of all tactical and strategic representations of warfare for the soldier, the tank or aircraft pilot, and above all the senior officer who engages combat forces.

Leaving aside the systematic use of simulators in preparations for land, sea and air missions, we should also mention the radical change in nuclear deterrence itself with the recent East–West disarmament initiatives. The gradual elimination of medium- and short-range 'theatre' weapons, and their replacement by light, 'smart' missiles such as the Midgetman, Stinger or Smart-Gun, are the harbingers of a final shift that will probably lead in turn to the disappearance of these latest weapons too. What will take their place will be directed-beam weapons using laser energy, charged particles or electro-magnetic forces, which will function at the speed of light, after the fashion of the high-resolution cameras aboard military observation satellites.

When that stage is reached, probably at the end of the century, the deterrence strategy geared to nuclear weapons will give way to one based upon ubiquitous orbital vision of enemy territory. Rather like in a Western gun-duel, where firepower equilibrium is less important than reflex response, eyeshot will then finally get the better of gunshot. It will be an optical, or electro-optical, confrontation; its likely slogan, 'winning is keeping the target in constant sight'. 'Winning' here means the status quo of a new balance of forces, based not on explosives and delivery systems but on the instant power of sensors, interceptors and remote electronic detectors. As Merleau-Ponty once wrote: 'The problem of knowing who is the subject of the state and war will be of exactly the same kind as the problem of knowing who is the subject of perception.' However, it is not human observers or military analysts themselves who will have this ubiquitous and surgically precise vision: rather, a 'sight machine' aboard an intelligent satellite will automate perception of enemy territory in the finest detail, helping the missile's 'expert system' to reach its decision at the speed of electronic circuitry.

With this assumption of cybernetics into the heavens, we seem to have moved far away from military cinematography. Yet the innovation of eyeless vision is directly descended from the history of the line of aim. The act of taking aim is a geometrification of looking, a way of technically aligning ocular perception along an imaginary axis that used to be known in French as the 'faith line' (ligne de foi). Prefiguring the numerical optics of a computer that can recognize shapes, this 'line of aim' anticipated the automation of perception – hence the obligatory reference to faith, belief, to denote the ideal alignment of a look which, starting from the eye, passed through the peep-hole and the sights and on to the target object. Significantly, the word 'faith' is no longer used in this context in contemporary French: the ideal line appears thoroughly objective, and the semantic loss involves a new obliviousness to the element of interpretative subjectivity that is always in play in the act of looking.

If we tried to write a history of this 'line of force', of this perceptual 'faith', it would have to take account of quite a few vicissitudes, particularly since the invention of photography in the first half of the nineteenth century, followed by cinema, and then by videos, computer graphics and the *active optics* of the synthetic image.

By the seventeenth century the emergence of the astronomical telescope had revolutionized the way in which the world was seen, and this 'faith line' had been broken or refracted in the *passive optics* of Galileo's lenses. In fact, by upsetting geocentric cosmogony, this reverberation of the human look called perceptual faith itself into question, and 'remote perception' anticipated the grave philosophical problems that have recently been posed by 'electro-optical television', as a preliminary to a new science of 'visionics' concerned with the automated interpretation of reality. Thus, alongside the 'war machine', there has always existed an ocular (and later optical and electro-optical) 'watching machine' capable of providing soldiers, and particularly commanders, with a visual perspective on the military action under way. From the original watch-tower through the anchored balloon to the reconnaissance aircraft and remote-sensing satellites, one and the same function has been indefinitely repeated, the eye's function being the function of a weapon. However great the area of the battlefield, it is necessary to have the fastest possible access to pictures of the enemy's forces and reserves. Seeing and foreseeing therefore tend to merge so closely that the actual can no longer be distinguished from the potential. Military actions take place 'out of view', with radio-electrical images substituting in real time for a now failing optical vision.

Another recent innovation, going beyond infra-red thermal images, has been television that can operate in poor lighting conditions. The light-intensifying camera, for example, no longer simply takes pictures but can increase the surrounding level of light, behaving towards nocturnal photons in the manner of a particle accelerator. Like a lighthouse perforating the night, such television makes darkness transparent and gives to military contestants an image of what the night is no longer able to conceal. Thus, side by side with the thermal camera and radar technology, a new means of generating indirect light is tending to supplant the source of electric light. Electro-optical lighting is the fruit of the latest technology developed both for the army and for the police, who regularly use it at the exits from evening football matches.

The industrial production of repeating guns and automatic weapons was thus followed by the innovation of repeating images, with the photogram providing the occasion. As the video signal supplemented the classical radio signal, the video camera further extended such 'cinematography' and allowed the adversary to be kept under remote surveillance in real time, by day and by night.

'If I had to sum up current thinking on precision missiles and saturation weaponry in a single sentence,' said W.J. Perry, a former US Under-Secretary of State for Defense, 'I'd put it like this: once you can see the target, you can expect to destroy it.' This quotation perfectly expresses the new geostrategic situation and partially explains the current round of disarmament. If *what is perceived is already lost*, it becomes necessary to invest in concealment what used to be invested in simple exploitation of one's available forces – hence the spontaneous generation of the new Stealth weapons. Research and development work on electronic counter-measures (decoys) now occupies a preponderant place in military–industrial undertakings. But it is itself a 'stealthy' place, censorship in this sphere going far beyond the old military secrecy which surrounded, for example, the invention of the atom bomb.

The inversion of the deterrence principle is quite clear: unlike weapons which have to be publicized if they are to have a real deterrent effect, Stealth equipment can only function if its existence is clouded with uncertainty. This 'aesthetics of disappearance' introduces a disturbing element of enigma into relations between the blocs, gradually calling into question the very nature of nuclear deterrence. The core of the Strategic Defense Initiative is not so much, as Reagan claims, the deployment of new weapons in space as the indeterminacy or unfamiliarity of a weapons system whose credibility is no more assured than its visibility.

We can now better understand the crucial importance of this 'logistics of perception' and of the secrecy that surrounds it. A war of pictures and sounds is replacing the war of objects (projectiles and missiles). In a tech-nicians' version of an all-seeing Divinity, ever ruling out accident and surprise, the drive is on for a general system of illumination that will allow everything to be seen and known, at every moment and in every place.

This first volume seeks to show the recent origins of this project and to follow the twists and turns of its development. A subsequent book will look more closely at the latest results in this domain.

Paul Virilio
30 March 1988

1

Military Force Is Based upon Deception*

When underground militants – Irish or Basque, Action Directe or Red Brigades – use outrages, murder or torture to gain publicity, feeding the media with photos of their sacrificial victims, the act of internal war throws back to its psychotropic origins in sympathetic magic, to the riveting spectacle of immolation and death agony, the world of ancient religions and tribal gatherings. Terrorism insidiously reminds us that war is a symptom of delirium operating in the half-light of trance, drugs, blood and unison. This half-light establishes a corporeal identity in the clinch of allies and enemies, victims and executioners – the clinch not of homosexual desire but of the antagonistic homogeneity of the death wish, a perversion of the right to live into a right to die.[1] 'War abounds with suggestions and hallucinations', writes General F. Gambiez. 'The search for psychological factors – whether depressive or tonic – helps to restore the true countenance of battle.'

Since Antiquity, military institutions have continued to revolutionize science and technology, and to solve the most complex and varied technical problems. But for all that they have never broken from the pre-scientific model, that moment in which war ceases to be just a science of the accidental. War can never break free from the magical spectacle because its very purpose is to *produce* that spectacle: to fell the enemy is not so much to capture as to 'captivate' him, to instil the fear of death before he actually dies. From Machiavelli to Vauban, from von Moltke to Churchill, at every decisive episode in the history of war, military theorists have underlined this truth: 'The force of arms is not brute force but spiritual force.'[2]

---

*Sun Tzu

There is no war, then, without representation, no sophisticated weaponry without psychological mystification. Weapons are tools not just of destruction but also of perception – that is to say, stimulants that make themselves felt through chemical, neurological processes in the sense organs and the central nervous system, affecting human reactions and even the perceptual identification and differentiation of objects. A well-known example is the *Stuka* or Junker 87, the German dive-bomber of World War Two that swept down on its target with a piercing screech designed to terrorize and paralyse the enemy. It was completely successful in this aim until the forces on the ground eventually grew used to it.

In this respect the first atomic bombs, dropped on Hiroshima and Nagasaki on the 6th and 9th of August 1945, presented the ideal conditions: great mechanical effectiveness, complete technical surprise, but, above all, the moral shock that suddenly banished to the prop-room the earlier strategic carpet-bombing of large Asian and European cities, with all its logistical sluggishness. By demonstrating that they would not recoil from a civilian holocaust, the Americans triggered in the minds of the enemy that *information explosion* which Einstein, towards the end of his life, thought to be as formidable as the atomic blast itself.[3] The principle of deterrence had already seen the light of day.

The term *credibility*, so often used with reference to nuclear weapons, tells us a great deal about the real nature of the balance of terror. In fact the idea of such a balance, originally hailed as a divine gift by the Americans, has more to do with dogma than with any strategic theory.[4] As Marshal Grechko, Brezhnev's defence minister, put it: 'Continual development of our armed forces is an *objective necessity* for the construction of socialism and communism.' In other words, even when weapons are not employed, they are active elements of ideological conquest.

This nuclear faith, however, is beginning to waver and to encounter its first heretics. A number of generals are now saying that, after all, 'a nuclear conflict would not be the end of the world', repeating twenty years later the argument of General Buck Turgidson in Stanley Kubrick's *Dr Strangelove*: 'I don't say we wouldn't get our hair mussed, Mr President, but only ten to twenty million casualties – depending on the breaks.'[5] The balance of terror is changing because now everyone, or nearly everyone, has the bomb: in accustoming ourselves to nuclear sabre-rattling we have the illusion of reaching a new stage of knowledge. Illustrating, at a perceptual level, Lord Mountbatten's motto 'when it works it's out of date', a 'new Hiroshima' would today be just a trivial remake, an 'explosion of mini-bombs expressed merely in kilotonnes', as the military experts like to joke. Ronald Reagan understood this perfectly when he reopened the debate on 23 March 1983, unveiling a plan to establish a space-based anti-ballistic-missile system relying on lasers and mirrors . . .

all by the year 2000. Most of the specialists who were asked about the project immediately talked of it as Star Wars, science-fiction cinema. But the necessary element of spectacle has behind it a thoroughly concrete programme on which the Pentagon will spend around a billion dollars a year. Similarly, while the stockpiling of weapons that will doubtless never be used is considered by the uninitiated to be an act of madness, in military eyes not only is it not an aberration, its magic is precisely to be without any justification, to have no other reason for existence than to be brandished and quantified in public. Since, according to J.P. Goebbels, the only measure of a military decision lies in its monstrous power, the very disproportion in the published figures (kilotonnes per head of population, etc.) serves to counteract the sense of familiarity among the populations in question and to stir up their nuclear faith. In order to create a climate of terror, military men in both camps will certainly have to come up with something better than the forty million killed in the Second World War. This is why President Carter, continuing in a sense Eisenhower's last speech in 1961 that attacked the military–industrial complex, declared in his farewell address to the nation:

> It may only be a matter of time before madness, desperation, greed or mis-calculation lets loose this terrible force. In an all-out nuclear war, more destructive power than in all of World War Two would be unleashed every second during the long afternoon it would take for all the missiles and bombs to fall. *A World War Two every second* – more people killed in the first few hours than in all the wars of history put together.[6]

It is an arms race in which the doctrine and delirium of production have gradually replaced the doctrine of battlefield use, and the element of surprise – coming, as it did in the Malvinas war of 1982, from the technology itself rather than from the politicians, armies or general staffs – affects both adversaries at once. Battle is now nothing more than the autonomy, or automation, of the war machine, with its virtually undetectable 'smart' weapons such as the Exocet missile, the Beluga bomb, the Tigerfish torpedo, the 'Raygun Project' of lightning nuclear attack being studied by the Pentagon, the Doomsday machine . . .

From the first missiles of World War Two to the lightning flash of Hiroshima, the *theatre weapon* has replaced the *theatre of operations*. Indeed the military term 'theatre weapon', though itself outmoded, underlines the fact that *the history of battle is primarily the history of radically changing fields of perception*. In other words, war consists not so much in scoring territorial, economic or other material victories as in appropriating the 'immateriality' of perceptual fields. As belligerents set out to invade those fields in their totality, it became apparent that the true war film did not necessarily have to depict war or any actual battle. For once the cinema was able to create surprise (technological, psychological, etc.), it effectively came under the category of weapons.

Thus it was no accident that colour films multiplied during the Second World War – indeed, in Germany they were the direct result of acts of logistical piracy. Early in the war Joseph Goebbels, minister for propaganda and 'patron' of the German cinema, banned the showing of the first film in Agfacolor, *Women Are Better Diplomats (Frauen Sind Doch Bessere Diplomaten)*, on the grounds that the colour was depressing and of wretched quality. In fact, he had had the opportunity to see very recent American films – particularly *Gone with the Wind* – which the German navy had salvaged from intercepted Allied ships. Compared with the American Technicolor, the German process struck Goebbels as nothing short of *shameful*. Shortly afterwards, Agfacolor was improved, mainly through the efforts of Eduard Schönicke, one of the directors of the famous IG-Farben company. In 1942 Veit Harlan, director of *The Jew Süss*, shot *The Golden City (Die Goldene Stadt)* with the new colour stock and it enjoyed enormous success in occupied Europe. In 1943, to mark ten years of Nazi cinema and the twenty-fifth anniversary of UFA (Universal Aktion Film), J. von Baky solemnly presented *The Adventures of Baron Münchhausen*, a high-budget Agfacolor film with a large number of very accomplished special effects. It was an act of war which enabled S.M. Eisenstein to shoot a long sequence of *Ivan the Terrible, Part Two* with captured Agfacolor stock. We should recall here that UFA had been founded during the First World War, in 1917, and that in the following year it became the main complex of cinematographic production, distribution and development in wartime Germany. Although enjoying state subsidies, it was from the beginning dependent on high finance, principally on Krupp and the arms industry.

At the height of total war, it seemed to Goebbels and to Hitler himself that the rescuing of the German cinema from black-and-white would provide it with a competitive edge against the tonic power of American productions. In short, the war justified Goethe's remark in his theory of colours:

> Colours have a strange duplicity and, if I may be allowed to express myself so, a kind of dual hermaphroditism, a peculiar way of attracting, associating and mixing with one other, of neutralizing and cancelling one another, etc. Moreover, they produce physiological, pathological and aesthetic effects that continue to frighten.

One day when I was discussing with my wife this powerful mimetic faculty of American cinema, she said that what she had found most unbearable in the Nazi occupation of France was the feeling of being cut off from the United States. At a stroke there would be no more American magazines, no more newspapers, above all, no more movies. In her child's universe, the cinema was a kind of 'perceptual luxury' (Bergson) quite distinct from other forms of spectacle and entertainment, an abstract weekly luxury which it would be very hard for her to do without. The Nazi leaders understood this very well: they placed actors and directors under military discipline right from the outbreak of hostilities, any absence from the studios being regarded as an act of desertion and punished accordingly. In fact, Goebbels had a contemptuous relationship with the cinema people, many of whom had very little conviction in the Nazi cause. Some were Communists, others were Jews or married to Jewish women and eventually met a tragic end: Hans Meyer-Hanno and Joachim Gottschalk, for example; or UFA's chief electrician Fritz Kühne and his Jewish wife Loni, who died by their own hands in 1944 rather than be separated by her deportation.[7]

Such were the coercive means by which high-budget films continued to be produced right up to the end of the war. When all the cinemas lay in ruins in the bombed cities of the Reich, new films were still being screened in the last Nazi outposts. *Kolberg*, for instance, was made in 1943–44 at a cost of eight-and-a-half million marks – eight times the normal budget for a major film – but could not have its première until 30 January 1945, in the Atlantic fortress of La Rochelle, still in German hands.

We shall come back to the extraordinary circumstances under which *Kolberg* was filmed. Let us just note here that Goebbels, staring military collapse in the face, had wanted the film to be 'the greatest of all time, a spectacular epic outrivalling the most sumptuous American super-productions'.[8] Once again we see Goebbels's obsession with the American perceptual arsenal, fragments of which he could still obtain relatively easily in the shape of magazines, newspapers and films. For we should not forget that, apart from the pickings of secret agents and distinguished travellers, the diplomatic mail, prisoner-of-war correspondence and the international press continued to pass more or less discreetly from one side to the other by means of the 'tolerated' air links. Thus, daily services operated between London, Lisbon, Stockholm and Switzerland, providing invaluable sources of information for both Allied and German belligerents, whose national airliners stood side by side on the runways of neutral countries.

In the United States itself, cinema production was watched closely by the military High Command – when, that is, the Pentagon did not take direct charge of the production and release of propaganda films. There too, careers followed ambivalent courses – John Huston and Anatole Litvak being two of the best-known instances. Rather unexpectedly, Luis Buñuel could be found in 1942 shooting documentaries for the US Army, while Frank Capra moved from his inter-war satires (most notably with

Harry Langdon) to the ponderous didacticism of *Why We Are Fighting*
(1942–45) and, more straightforwardly still, the songs and dances of Fred
Astaire became disguised calls for a new mobilization.

The aggressive colours of these films – long considered by Europeans,
and particularly the French, to be a mark of 'bad taste' – made them into
veritable 'war paintings' whose task was to imbue audiences with fresh
energy, to wrench them out of apathy in the face of danger or distress, to
overcome that wide-scale demoralization which was so feared by generals
and statesmen alike. In the United States, the magic of arms directly
revived the magic of the market, as total war succeeded the economic
warfare of the New Deal thirties. By 1946, the year after Hiroshima, Fred
Astaire was singing to *Blue Skies*, skies that were at once luminous and
laden with gloom, technicolor skies of the kind so often seen during the
war, distantly reflecting the inexpressible melancholy of those, within the
ruins, who had in the end survived the mourning and the rubble. As the
Cold War set in around 1950, followed by Korea and then Vietnam,
Roosevelt's policies were abandoned for ever. The old propaganda movies
(beginning with *Why We Are Fighting*) were withdrawn from circulation,
the convalescent joy of the immediate post-war period was gradually
extinguished. With mass demobilization the order of the day, the great
American musical comedy ceased to exist, deprived by nuclear deterrence
of its noble aspirations and its military–political requisites.[9]

According to Napoleon, *the capacity for war is the capacity for movement*. In the nineteenth century, the development of military psychology
coincided exactly with the rise of physiology and experimental psychology. E.J. Marey, himself a medical physiologist and disciple of Claude
Bernard, placed the chronophotography that he had invented at the
service of military research into movement. Fred Astaire's persistent *charm*
doubtless stems from this unsuspected fusion/confusion of 'science' and
dance. The thin and glittering hem of his tuxedo, his dancing exaltation of
the most everyday steps and body-movements, call to mind that 'hijack-
ing' of the spectator's gaze of which Marey was so fond. When he photographed the movement of white birds or horses, or human subjects with
silver strips on their black clothing, he was making the body disappear
into a momentary agglomeration of sense-data, oscillating between the
production of luminous impressions and that pure fascination which
dispels perceptual awareness and induces hypnosis or similar pathological
conditions.[10]

In short, it is not surprising that the tap-dancing of the thirties, forties
and fifties – pirated from Marey's magnetoscope and absorbed in high
doses – should still work today. Overexposure to those images, so full of
thoughts and *arrière-pensées*, remains one of the best remedies there are
against the dark.

2

Cinema Isn't I See, It's I Fly*

It was in 1861, whilst travelling on a paddle-steamer and watching its wheel, that the future Colonel Gatling hit upon the idea of a cylindrical, crank-driven machine-gun. In 1874 the Frenchman Jules Janssen took inspiration from the multi-chambered Colt (patented in 1832) to invent an astronomical revolving unit that could take a series of photographs. On the basis of this idea, Etienne-Jules Marey then perfected his chrono-photographic rifle, which allowed its user to aim at and photograph an object moving through space.

It was partly thanks to information provided by the *Entrepreneur*, the first battlefield observation balloon, that General Jourdan won the victory of Fleurus in 1794. In 1858 Nadar took his first pictures from a balloon. During the American Civil War, the Union forces equipped balloons with an aerial-mapping telegraph. Soon the army was rigging together the most varied combinations: camera-kites, camera-pigeons and camera-balloons predated the intensive use of chronophotography and cinematography on board small reconnaissance aircraft (several million prints were made during the First World War). By 1967 the US Air Force had the whole of South-East Asia covered, and pilotless aircraft would fly over Laos and send their data back to IBM centres in Thailand or South Vietnam. *Direct vision was now a thing of the past*: in the space of a hundred and fifty years, the target area had become a cinema 'location', the battlefield a film set out of bounds to civilians.

During the First World War, D.W. Griffith was the only American film-maker authorized to go to the front to shoot propaganda footage for the Allies. Son of a Civil War veteran, Griffith had previously worked in the

---

*Paraphrase of Nam June Paik

11

theatre and, in the summer of 1914, had filmed the great battle scenes of
Birth of a Nation just as Europe was plunging into a real war. In this film,
the battlefield appears in a long-distance shot taken from a hilltop, the
director being in the position of Pierre Bezukhov, the hero of King Vidor's
and Mario Soldati's *War and Peace* (1955), as he contemplates the fighting at Borodino with all the risks of direct vision. In fact Griffith filmed
'his war' less as an epic painter than in the style of those stage-managers
who meticulously note down the slightest movement to be performed in
the theatre. Karl Brown has related: 'Every gun emplacement was known.
Every motion of every section of the crowd. I say section, because each
section was put under a sub-director – one of Griffith's many assistants –
Victor Fleming, Joseph Henabery, Donald Crisp.'[1] All the action was
organized not by megaphone (since nothing would have been heard above
the explosions and blank rifle-fire) but through variously coloured
pennants relaying a kind of naval semaphore. 'Take away the crowd
scenes,' writes Kevin Brownlow,

> and any of today's home movie enthusiasts could duplicate the conditions
> under which *Birth of a Nation* was made. Infinitely more labour-saving devices
> are at his fingertips than were available to Griffith and his cameraman Billy
> Bitzer. They used no lights – Bitzer employed mirrors to bounce the sun
> around. There were no exposure meters or zoom lenses or lightweight cameras.
> Just a heavy wooden Pathé, sturdy and well designed, cranked by hand. Yet
> photographically it was outstanding, and the direction was often inspired.[2]

Towards the end of the nineteenth century, Billy Bitzer had made what
were known as 'motion demonstrations' – short music-hall films inspired
by the Lumière brothers – and had then been sent to Cuba on behalf of the
American Mutoscope Company at the height of the Spanish–American
War. But although, as early as 1898, the ingenious Bitzer had strapped his
Mutograph camera to the buffers of a locomotive travelling at full speed,
the cinema he made with Griffith still belonged to the world of the
Lumières' *Salon Indien*, where, in 1895, they first showed their *L'Arrivée
du train en gare de la Ciotat*. In other words, he looked from a stationary
outside at objects moving before him: the camera reproduced the circumstances of ordinary vision, as a homogeneous witness of the action.
Although his images have an inbuilt time-lag, their power lies in the
illusion of proximity they give to the spectator within a coherent temporal
unity.

It is well known that many film-makers, in order to avoid as much cutting as possible at the editing stage, used to rehearse the whole film from
beginning to end, timing each scene so that the total length would be
approximately known in advance. This method of shooting, quite

common in Germany in the twenties, influenced directors like Carl Dreyer, who would strive to create an *artificial* unity of time by means of a *real* unity of place, thereby illustrating Walter Benjamin's observation about a kind of cinema which was able to 'present an object for simultaneous collective experience, as it was possible for architecture at all times'.[3] This 'at all times' of architecture dominated the early twentieth-century cinema, particularly in Europe. Cinema light is not opposed to the opacity of architectural matter (of the camera obscura); it is only, like electricity, an unexpected technical measure of its duration, *a new daylight*. And architecture resists the nihilism of the shooting camera as the ramparts of a fortress, five hundred years earlier, resisted the fitful flickerings of artillery before they were destroyed by the shattering development of its projective power.

At the end of the last century Oskar Messter, not having a camera, used the room in which he lived as a camera obscura by blacking it out and leaving only a tiny hole at the street side. He then used his projector as a mechanical device to draw across the unexposed film. Messter came before the *Kammerspiel* theorists like Lupu Pick, who believed that the 'unbearable pressure of time and place' could replace the psychology of actors. In 1925 Dreyer shot *Master of the House* in the smallest possible space, a two-room abode scrupulously reconstituted as a cinema studio. Two years later, he made *Joan of Arc* on a single set – a truly compact piece of architecture at the city limits of Paris – and his chronological sequence of shooting coincided with that of the actual trial. One thinks also of Edison's famous tar-paper hut, the 'Black Maria' – another camera obscura – which served as both studio and projection room, capable of revolving on its pivot base so that its opening roof would trap the maximum amount of sunlight.

Chrono-logical development gradually did away with the *longueurs* of the old photographic pose; the architecture of the set, with its spatial mass and partitions, supplanted free montage and created a new narrative ellipsis. Rather like my grand-daughter, who, when she moved from one room of her flat to another, used to think that a different sun was shining into each one, so the cinema marked the advent of an independent and still unknown cycle of light. And if it was so hard for the photograph to move, this was above all because the operation of moving cinematic time – of perceiving its original speed in an old, static and rigidly ordered environment – was as astonishing for those early pioneers as it was difficult to invent.[4]

When the engineer Joseph Cugnot invented self-propulsive haulage in the eighteenth century, his main way of demonstrating it was to launch his army trolley against a wall with destructive impact. Curiously enough, a century later the Lumière brothers demonstrated *cinematic self-propulsion* by projecting a film called *Demolition of a Wall*. In the first part the wall collapsed in a cloud of dust; then the scene was projected in reverse, and the reconstitution of the wall introduced trick photography to the world of the cinema. Méliès also liked to perform this ritual of accidental destruction: in *Voyage à travers l'impossible*, for instance, which was made in 1904, the 'automaboulof' belonging to experts from the Institute of Incoherent Geography resumes the work of Cugnot's trolley by smashing down the wall of an inn. The next shot, inside the inn, shows the customers dining peacefully before the event – as if the wall had nevertheless absorbed cinematic time. In the years to come, directors would not hesitate to move from one setting to another, making their actors glide through walls. Doors would open in houses without a facade, so that the cross-sectioned partitions between rooms appeared as thin as the chinks between frames on the film.

In this way, film directors showed that they paid little attention to shifts in cinematic time, to the fact that even in a confined architectural space the whole problem is one of speed. For a camera motor works by holding back its potential energies, much as those schoolchildren of Pagnol's avoided playing in their tiny recreation ground so that it would appear larger to them.

Towards the end of the First World War, when Griffith arrived at the French front to make his propaganda film, the last romantic battle had long since taken place, in 1914 on the Marne. The war had become a static conflict in which the main action was for millions of men to hold fast to their piece of land, camouflaging themselves for months on end (years in cases like Verdun) amid a fearful proliferation of cemeteries and charnel-houses. With his experience of filming old-style battles, Griffith suddenly found himself out of his depth in events that depended on the breathtaking advance of new and unfamiliar technologies and placed greater emphasis on the means than on the ends.

To the naked eye, the vast new battlefield seemed to be composed of nothing – no more trees or vegetation, no more water or even earth, no hand-to-hand encounters, no visible trace of the unity of homicide and suicide. Between the German and Allied trenches, separated by a mere sixty or eighty metres, the famous slogan 'they shall not pass' took on a new meaning as literally no one passed across the field of vision. Numerous veterans from the 1914–18 war have said to me that although they killed enemy soldiers, at least they did not see whom they were killing, since others had now taken responsibility for seeing in their stead. What was this abstract zone that Apollinaire accurately described as the site of a blind, non-directional desire? The soldiers themselves could identify it only by the flight-path of their bullets and shells ('*Mon désir est là sur quoi je tire*'⁵), a kind of telescopic tensing towards an imagined encounter, a 'shaping' of the partner-cum-adversary before his probable fragmentation. As sight lost its direct quality and reeled out of phase, the soldier had the feeling of being not so much destroyed as derealized or dematerialized, any sensory point of reference suddenly vanishing in a surfeit of optical targets. Being constantly in the enemy's sights, he came to resemble Pirandello's cinema actors, in exile both from the stage and from themselves, who had to make do with acting in front of a little machine that then acted with their shadows for the audience:

> They are confusedly aware, with a maddening, indefinable sense of emptiness, that their bodies are so to speak subtracted, suppressed, deprived of their reality, of breath, of voice, of the sound that they make in moving about, to become only a dumb image, which quivers for a moment on the screen and disappears, in silence.⁶

Just as the nitrocellulose that went into film stock was also used for the production of explosives, so the artilleryman's motto was the same as the cameraman's: lighting reveals everything. By 1 October 1914 anti-aircraft artillery was already combining guns with searchlights. By 1918 the British Home Defence, for example, had not only eleven fighter squadrons but 284 anti-aircraft guns and 377 searchlight installations. On 9 January 1915, when the Kaiser ordered the first bombing attacks on London and its industrial suburbs, the British anti-aircraft defence was capable of producing remarkable films of the Zeppelin night raids. Whereas civilian cinematography lagged behind and remained largely dependent on sunlight, the Tsarist armed forces were already using searchlights to defend Port Arthur in 1904, and it would not be long before these were hitched to camera-machineguns.

Griffith declared that he was 'very disappointed with the reality of the battlefield'. And everything indicates that modern warfare had become incompatible with the art of cinema as both he and his audiences still conceived it. Nevertheless, he and his cameraman Captain Kleinschmidt shot some interesting footage of mainly logistical activity on the front, which can still be seen at the Imperial War Museum in London. Griffith then moved to England to re-create battles that were actually taking place a few hundred kilometres away. *Hearts of the World* (1918) was partly shot on Salisbury Plain, which later served as a 'special cemetery' for victims of the influenza epidemic that claimed twenty-seven million more lives throughout the world in the space of a year. Griffith then returned to Hollywood to complete the film on the Lasky ranch, with von Stroheim as his military adviser but with a quite limited budget. Despite its banal script, it was a big success in the United States and had a considerable impact on public opinion.

In the face of modern warfare, Griffith doubtless felt the same kind of bitterness that he had already experienced in watching Pastrone's *Cabiria*, which was begun in Italy in 1912 and reached America in 1914. According to Karl Brown, 'the reviews of *Cabiria* had such an effect on Griffith that he and key members of his staff took the next train to San Francisco to see it.' And Brownlow adds:

To have made a film hailed as the world's greatest masterpiece must have been exhilarating; but then to see a film like *Cabiria* must have been immeasurably depressing. Not that it exceeded the standard of *The Birth* [of a Nation] in terms of story, but in terms of physical production and technical dexterity, it made *The Birth* look primeval.[7]

Cabiria came from the land of the Futurists, whose manifesto had appeared three years earlier. For both Pastrone and the Futurists, the linear-Euclidian organization of thought had come to an end, human sight was on the same footing as energetic propulsion. Quite intentionally, Pastrone downplayed the element of plot in favour of technical effects and the dynamic improvement of cinema photography: 'Obsessed by the third dimension, director Giovanni Pastrone (under the pseudonym Piero Fosco) created shots of remarkable depth, separating the planes with a constantly moving camera.'[8] In refining and often misusing the *carello* or travelling shot, Pastrone showed that the camera's function was less to produce images (as painters and photographers had long been doing) than to manipulate and falsify dimensions.

'In order to create a dream-like effect – that is, visual hallucination,' states Ray Harryhausen, a contemporary master of special effects, 'it is no more necessary to copy "cinema motion" than a painter copies a photo- graph.'[9] This remark poses a clear-cut problem: cinema-truth may be produced twenty-four times a second by the motor of the camera, but the first difference between cinema and photography is that the viewpoint can be mobile, can get away from the static focus and share the speed of moving objects. Ever since Marey's experiments, the shooting camera had been mobile – stability had no longer implied fixity. After Pastrone, however, what was 'false' in cinema was no longer the effect of acceler- ated perspective but the very depth itself, the temporal distance of the projected space. Many years later, the electronic light of laser holography and integrated-circuit computer graphics would confirm this relativity in which speed appears as the primal magnitude of the image and thus the source of its depth.

Pastrone's film was made at the time of the colonial war in Libya, which was one of the consequences of the patriotic delirium and industrial–military expansion that had gripped Italy after the fiftieth anni- versary of national unification. Gabriele d'Annunzio, who collaborated on the script of *Cabiria*, was himself a bellicose dandy close to the Futurists who became a war pilot and went on to play a key role in the capture of Fiume.[10] It is strange that cinematic self-propulsion counted for so little in Futurist activity – just two films, in 1914 and 1916, one of which Marinetti dismissed as worthless – even though Marinetti himself was beginning to join together war, aviation and a vision which, in its fleeting aerial perspective, might be called 'dromoscopic'.[11] In 1912 he published *The Pope's Monoplane*, the account of a trip by a Futurist aviator, and almost simultaneously *The Battle of Tripoli*, inspired by his enthusiastic period on the Libyan front. In this latter book, the author's hand 'seems to detach itself from the body and to stretch out in freedom, a long way from the brain which, itself somehow detached from the now aerial body, looks down from a great height, and with a terrible lucidity, on the unexpected phrases flowing from the pen.'

At the turn of the century, cinema and aviation seemed to form a single moment. By 1914, aviation was ceasing to be strictly a means of flying and breaking records (the *Deperdussin* had already passed the 200 km.p.h. barrier in 1913); it was becoming one way, or perhaps even the ultimate way, of *seeing*. In fact, contrary to what is generally thought, the air arm grew out of the reconnaissance services, its military value having initially been questioned by the general staffs. Indeed the recon-naissance aircraft itself, whose function was to supply ground troops with information, to direct artillery barrages or to take photographs, gained acceptance merely as a 'flying observation post', almost as static as the old balloon with its cartographers, pencils and paper. Mobile information remained the province of the deep-penetrating cavalry until Joffre, at the Battle of the Marne, turned to the aviators for the first time in deciding on the offensive dispositions necessary for victory. The lot of the airborne crews was not an enviable one, since they had to maintain a constant alti-tude and thus expose themselves to enemy fire in order that the photo-graphic scale should remain the same. Jean Renoir belonged to one of these reconnaissance squadrons, and when he was filming *La Grande Illusion* he asked Jean Gabin to wear his old flying jacket from the war. 'The plot of *La Grande Illusion*', Renoir recalls,

was absolutely authentic; it was told to me by a number of comrades from the '14–18 war, particularly Pinsard. He was with the fighters, while I was in reconnaissance. Sometimes I had to go off and take pictures of the German lines. On several occasions he saved my life when the German fighters were becoming too insistent. He was brought down seven times, was imprisoned seven times, and escaped seven times.

Once the general staffs began to take aviation seriously, aerial reconnaissance, both tactical and strategic, became chronophotographic and then cinematographic. Although the aircraft had direct contact with the ground by means of wireless telegraphy, the considerable time needed to analyse the photographic information created a lag between the taking of pictures and their reinsertion into military activity.

Really exceptional pilots were few and far between. First there were the 'sporting types' like Védrines and Pégoud; then recruits started to come from all the other arms, particularly the specialist cavalry. At the start of the war pilots preferred to fly alone, but they had to perform extraordinary feats to keep navigating, filming and often firing as well. This tended to attract innovative minds – people like Roland Garros (d. 1918), whose machine-gun could be safely synchronized to fire through the propeller, or Omer Locklear, who earned his reputation in the Air Corps by climbing onto the wing of a moving aircraft and so proving that it could bear the weight of an extra machine-gun. In 1919 he began a Hollywood career as a stunt-flyer, just like Roland Toutain in France (the sentimental aviator of *La Règle du Jeu*). Another war pilot, Howard Hawks, won the financial backing of Howard Hughes in 1930 to make *The Dawn Patrol*, based on his own experiences in the war.

In July 1917 Manfred von Richthofen, the famous 'Red Baron', introduced his tactic of the 'flying circus' – wing formations containing four squadrons of eighteen aircraft each. In principle there was no longer an above or below, no longer any visual polarity. War pilots already had their own special effects, which they called 'looping', 'falling-leaf roll', 'figure of eight', and so on. Airborne vision now escaped that Euclidian neutralization which was so acutely felt by ground troops in the trenches; it opened endoscopic tunnels and even brought 'blind spots' within the most astounding topological field – vistas whose precursors could be found in the big wheels and other fairground attractions of the nineteenth century, and which were later developed in the roller-coasters and scenic railways of post-war funfairs, especially in Berlin.

In Vietnam, after forty years of stagnation, the Americans were quick to see the importance of rethinking problems of aerial observation. A technological revolution gradually pushed back the limits of investigation into space and time until aerial reconnaissance, with its old modes of representation, disappeared in instantaneous, 'real-time' information. Objects and bodies were forgotten as their physiological traces became accessible to a host of new devices – sensors capable of detecting vibrations, sounds and smells; light-enhancing television cameras, infra-red flashes, thermographic pictures that identified objects by their temperature, and so on. When time-lags were lost in real time, real time itself broke the constraints of chronology and became cinematic. No longer frozen as in an old photograph, military information allowed the past or the future to be interpreted, since human activity always gives off heat and light and can thus be extrapolated in time and space. In 1914, however, systematic aerial cover of the battlefield was still at the mercy of darkness, fog or low cloud. Only bombers had already freed themselves from the alternation of night and day: they began with simple electric lamps and were later fitted with spotlights under their wing-tips or landing gear.

The pattern of this research, in which lighting and climate set the rhythm and airborne and terrestrial vision are dominant by turns, forms the dialectical web of Losey's little-known film *Figures in a Landscape* (1970). Just like a Civil Defence or Traffic Police helicopter, the machine tracking Losey's two fugitives superimposes landscape pictures of the West. Combat here is a game in which all the instruments take part in the saturation of space. Those who conduct the hunt visually are concerned to annul distance, first on board their means of transport, then with their guns. As for the escapees, they use their weapons not so much to destroy as to establish a distance: they live only in what separates them from their pursuers, they can survive only through pure distance, their ultimate protection is the continuity of nature as a whole. Avoiding roads, houses and anything that points to human uses, the two men coil up in creases of the land, seek out the cover of grass and trees, atmospheric disturbances, and darkness. It is useful to recall that *Figures in a Landscape* was made at the height of the Vietnam War, when the First Cavalry Division – the same that once chased Indians across the Great Plains – was carrying out its traditional missions in combat helicopters. Ten years later, Coppola drew extensively on Losey's film to stage the helicopter ballets of *Apocalypse Now*, following the rhythm of a Western and using a bugle call to sound the charge of a cavalry squadron.

When commercial flights began again in 1919, often using converted bombers like the Bréguet-14, aerial vision became a widespread phenomenon with a large public. Right from the beginning, however, aerial photography had posed the problem of knowing which, in the technical mix of 'chrono/camera/aircraft/weapon', would gain the upper hand in the making of the war film, and whether the topological freedom due to the speed of the engine, and later to its firepower, did not create new cinematic facts incomparably more powerful than those of the camera motor. 'I still remember *the effect I produced* on a small group of Galla tribesmen massed around a man in black clothes,' reported Mussolini's son during the Abyssinian war of 1935–36. 'I dropped an aerial torpedo right in the centre, and the group opened up just like a flowering rose.'[12] In this account, the action of the weapon (dive-bomber) is described as subversive: one form suddenly dissolves before the war pilot's eyes, and in an extraordinary fade-out/fade-in another form appears and reconstitutes itself. He has created it, just as a director working on a viewer can edit a scene in an aesthetically pleasing manner.

Since the battlefield has always been a field of perception, the war machine appears to the military commander as an instrument of representation, comparable to the painter's palette and brush. As is well known, great importance was attached to pictorial representation in the Oriental military sects, the warrior's hand readily passing from brush to sword. Similarly, the pilot's hand automatically trips the camera shutter with the same gesture that releases his weapon. *For men at war, the function of the weapon is the function of the eye.* It is therefore quite understandable that, after 1914, the air arm's violent cinematic disruption of the space continuum, together with the lightning advances of military technology, should have literally exploded the old homogeneity of vision and replaced it with the heterogeneity of perceptual fields. At that time, explosion metaphors were widely used in both art and politics. Film-makers who survived the war moved without any break in continuity from the battlefield to the production of newsreels or propaganda features and then 'art films'. Dziga Vertov, who joined Lenin's first agit-prop train in 1918, had this to say about the film-maker's 'armed eye':

I am the camera's eye. I am the machine which shows you the world as I alone see it. Starting from today, I am forever free of human immobility. I am in perpetual movement. I approach and draw away from things – I crawl under them – I climb on them – I am on the head of a galloping horse – I burst at full speed into a crowd – I run before running soldiers – I throw myself down on my back – I rise up with the aeroplanes – I fall and I fly at one with the bodies falling or rising through the air.[13]

These film-makers, who seemed to 'hijack' the image as the surrealists hijacked language, were themselves merely being hijacked by war. On the battlefield not only did they become warriors, they thought that like airmen they formed part of a kind of technical elite. It was a final privilege of their art that the First World War showed them military technology in action, and interestingly enough this technological surprise triggered a potent fusion/confusion in 'avant-garde' productions of the immediate post-war period. While war footage or aerial chronophotography remained under lock and key or was simply shrugged aside (as it mainly was in the United States), film-makers served up the technological effects to the public as a novel spectacle, a continuation of the war's destruction of form.

Let us take the famous example of Colonel Steichen, who directed air-reconnaissance operations for the US expeditionary corps during the First World War.[14] Nearly 1,300,000 prints ended up in his private collection, and a good number of these were exhibited and sold as his personal property. With 55 officers and 1,111 men under his command, Steichen had relied on a division of labour and intensive production methods to organize a factory-style output of war information. The photograph thus ceased to be an episodic item, as Steichen turned out a veritable flow of pictures which fitted perfectly with the statistical tendencies of this first great military–industrial conflict. As in the case of D.W. Griffith, the pressure of the war arsenal on pictorial production (Ford's assembly-lines had come into operation in 1914) did not fail to revolutionize Steichen's ideas about photography.

Like most photographers, Edward Steichen was first and foremost a 'painter-photographer', fond of France and so admiring of Rodin that he attended his funeral in 1917. Steichen's own photographic self-portrait, depicting him with palette and brush, is quite plainly a 'camera replica' of Titian's *Man with a Glove*. American film-makers like De Mille or Griffith also took pleasure in such photographic 'responses' to well-known paintings. The journal *Camera Work*, which ceased publication just as the United States was entering the war in 1917, soundly rejected 'pictorialism' as an avant-garde method in its final issue. Steichen himself lost no time in immersing himself in his military duties. But after the Armistice he retired in utter dejection to his French country home, burned his canvases and swore never to paint again. Indeed he dismissed any pictorial inspiration as 'elitist' and based himself on the planning methods of aerial reconnaissance in order to arrive at a redefinition of the image. With Steichen war photos became pictures of the 'American dream', soon to merge with those of the Hollywood system of industrial promotion and its codes for mass consumption.

In *Cahiers du cinéma*, Bergala once wrote: 'The star pin-up did not have to be invented . . . it was enough to *deepen the act of isolation* that the image of a star already involved in the great days of Hollywood.'[15] When I read this sentence, I think of the scene in Renoir's *La Grande Illusion* where the prisoners-of-war, in preparation for a *fête*, go through a collection of theatrical costumes and take out the faded instruments of feminine seduction. Intimate underwear, rustling petticoats are passed from hand to hand to the accompaniment of manic laughter and knowing gestures, until suddenly the men's faces cloud over as each individual withdraws in secret communion with himself, the Host being the very insubstantiality of that clothing cast off by women, who have disappeared in the separation of war. In a parallel sequence, a rich Jewish prisoner played by Marcel Dalio is offering a festive meal which embodies a further sense of apartness. Here too an indirect, non-logical form of perception is created, so that each prisoner ends up transferring his tastes, judgement and sense of things from being to figuration, from the form to its reflection. A general interpretation mania is thus imposed by the very facts of military logistics, for the soldier receives in his mail-packet the bare outlines of a meal rather than a meal itself, a lock but not a real head of women's hair. Renoir shows that even outside the field of battle – which never actually appears in the film – war subverts the proper experience of sex and death.

One is reminded here of Irma Pavolin, Maupassant's syphilitic young prostitute who delightedly totted up the numbers as she turned her sexuality into a means of waging bacteriological warfare on whole battalions of Prussian soldiers. Or take Henny Porten, the German cinema star who appeared in anti-French propaganda films and became one of the first known pin-ups to hang in the soldiers' quarters in 1914. The exemplary pin-up, representing an idealized young woman, took over the tradition of the carefully retouched photograph that serving soldiers used to receive from a female correspondent, a distant, intangible and often unknown fiancée of death who appeared only in letters containing, in addition to a few 'sweet nothings', such personal relics as a lock of hair, a glove, a trace of perfume or some dried flowers. Rudolf Arnheim once remarked that, after 1914, many film-actors became props while the props took the leading role. Similarly, women became *objective tragedy* in the wars from which they were excluded.

The leer that the conquering soldier casts on a woman's now-distant body is the same as that which he directs at a land turned into desert by war. It is also a direct antecedent of the cinematic voyeurism with which a director films the star as one does a landscape, with its lakes, contours and valleys. He alone has the task of 'lighting it up', thanks to a camera which, in the words of Marlene Dietrich's creator, Josef von Sternberg, 'hits at point-blank range'. (Many directors who were imported by the Americans after 1918 had served in the war, particularly in the Austro-Hungarian and German armies.) In more recent times Carol Reed told an aspiring actress: 'Being good isn't what counts; *the camera has to fall in love with you.*'[16] During and after the Second World War the widespread popularity of striptease, with its allusion to film as well as sexual excitation, indicated the scale of this technophiliac transfer in a society undergoing militarization. Overcoming censorship restrictions, it was imposed in Britain by the armed forces, particularly with the famous Phyllis Dixey. Like the soldier, the striptease dancer who undresses on stage becomes a film for spectators, slowly taking off her clothes in a series of takes in which her lascivious body-movements act as the overlapping dissolve and the music as the sound-track. This dimension has become even clearer in those shows where a glass-caged nude faces the customers through a 'screen', while they fire off their still- or cine-cameras 'at point-blank range'; or in those video-games which are considered 'won' when a small red light symbolizing orgasm appears on the screen within ninety seconds.[17]

Bergala's point about the actor's progressive isolation may thus be complemented by a quotation from Sydney Franklin: 'Every ounce of creative energy was harnessed to bring the star closer in every sense to the audience.' And he adds: 'You could take 1,000 feet of Norma Talmadge in a chair, and her fans would flock to see it.'[18] The star system and the sex symbol were the result of that unforeseen perceptual logistics which developed intensively in every field during the First World War. The United States, being nomadic by nature, secured the triumph of its own methods in a Europe still lacking in mobility and breadth of geographic vision. For example, the fact that America was able to field 20,000 tank wagons during the war, against France's 400, enabled it to win one of the first oil wars, as a result of which the French market effectively fell into the hands of Standard Oil. Clearly it was not so much consumption needs as the supply system itself that was now creating the market, and in the 1920s, long before the New Deal, the US media lost their neutrality as they fell under the control of industrial–commercial interests bent upon economic warfare. These powers kept a tight grip on Hollywood and those auxiliary industries which 'fanned out around the studios, as towns spread around castles'.[19]

In 1889 the circular terrace of the Eiffel Tower, with its floodlights and a telegraph office which opened to the public on the 9th of September, had greatly excited both Thomas Edison and a group of Indians from Buffalo Bill's 'Great Wild West Show'. But it was Lieutenant-Colonel Gustave Ferrié, a graduate of the Ecole Polytechnique, who first thought of using the tower as a giant aerial, and when war broke out in 1914 he was immediately given responsibility for the whole of radio-communications. On his initiative all the Allies' radiotelegraphic equipment was subsequently produced in France, and soon the old wireless telegraphy was transformed into a radio service. In 1915 the first electronic tube – the T.M. [military telegraphy] valve, invented by one of Ferrié's team – entered mass production, and by the end of the war people were already beginning to dream of television.

It is significant that the RKO logo was to be an outsized pylon whose purpose was no longer, like the Eiffel Tower, to 'astound the world' but to cover with messages a globe that it already dominated. To pictorial logistics (photographic or cinematographic) war added a logistics of sound and then of music, thanks to the 'popular radiophonics' which took off between the wars in huge auditoria and public broadcasts. 'Roses of Picardy' (1914) and 'Lili Marlene' (1940) are two wartime landmarks of the new musical logistics, while Glenn Miller, who came to a mysterious end, developed as one of its effective patrons. The ambivalence of these systems appeared clearly during the Blitz, with its nervous giggling, its cryptic musical arrangements conveying coded information to shadowy partisan fighters on the Continent. In Britain, the Ministry of Information housed a 'propaganda think-tank', one of whose best-known members was the actor Leslie Howard, star of *Gone with the Wind*. After his return from Hollywood in August 1939, he broadcast to the United States while an Englishman named William Joyce was addressing the British from Germany.

For his part Joseph Goebbels, that ex-journalist turned head of propaganda, had come up with many new ideas in the inter-war period. In helping Hitler to power, he had sent fifty thousand fascist propaganda records to gramophone-owning households and had forced cinema managers, often under threat of violence, to screen ideologically loaded shorts. Once he became a minister, he ensured that radio sets were within reach of everyone's pocket.

In 1914 it was still up to the pilot whether he wore a helmet, and his only means of 'insulation' were protective goggles and pieces of cotton-wool in the ears to muffle wind and engine noise. Some thirty years later, towards the end of the Second World War, the pressurized cockpits of US Superfortress bombers had become artificial synthesizers that shut out the world of the senses to a quite extraordinary degree. However, the effects of technological isolation were so severe and long-lasting that Strategic Air Command decided to lighten the dangerous passage of its armadas over Europe by painting brightly-coloured cartoon heroes or giant pin-ups with evocative names on top of the camouflage. In a kind of CB system, honey-tongued female announcers not only assumed radio guidance of the crews but also helped them through their mission by blurring the image of destruction with jokes, personal confidences and even songs of love.

Stanley Kubrick accurately reproduced this audio-visual effect when he used Vera Lynn's singing of 'We'll Meet Again' to soften the long series of nuclear explosions that conclude *Dr Strangelove*. Some reviewers criticized him for using old newsreel footage of Hiroshima or Christmas Island – inexpensive material which everyone had had the chance of seeing many times before.[20] But in fact Kubrick was motivated by the highest sense of realism, going straight to the heart of the war image. Here nothing is left but the recording of successive states of discharged matter and the record of a faraway voice which sings of the desire for reunion that has now become physically impossible, only this time for everyone and for evermore.

Through its hyper-generation of movement, mixing the accomplishments of the means of destruction and the means of communicating destruction, war falsifies appearance by falsifying distance. For the military commander, every dimension is unstable and presents itself in isolation from its natural context. Hermes, the god of all logistics, was baptised Trismegistus, three times great, as was the Egyptian god Thoth, while the *Iliad* has the 'giant' Achilles advancing to the walls of Troy. Conquerors such as Rameses or Stalin take the form of overblown stone or bronze colossi, seemingly capable of moving through an expanded, emptied world that no one had previously thought of as a field of action. In the same way, Gulliver or Alice would say: 'I've been changed several times.' But for Alice the visible world does not run up against the screen of the mirror; the luminous reflection is not a limit but a point of passage. Lewis Carroll, of course, was also the mathematician Charles Dodgson, co-inventor of a kind of mathematical logistics ('transcendental mathematics') in which continuity and discontinuity communicate with each other. He was also passionately keen on photography. The star system stemmed from this same instability of dimensions, which not everyone received with equanimity. Indeed, some audiences were quite disconcerted by the breaks in spatio-temporal continuity dreamt up by the film-makers.[21]

Again it is no accident that one of the last stars, Marilyn Monroe, was discovered by a US army photographer at the height of the Korean War. Nicknamed Miss Flamethrower (itself reminiscent of Marinetti's 'flame-women', 'lightning-carriages', 'engine-heart' and similar couplings), she earned 150 dollars a week and became the most popular pin-up on barrack-room walls. The power of Marilyn and her 'sisters' lay not only in their perfectly photogenic bodies but also in the fact that their pictures were not life-sized. Always in exile from its immediate, natural dimensions, never seeming to be connected to anything else, Marilyn's body was at once expandable like a giant screen and capable of being folded and reproduced like a poster, a magazine cover or a centre-spread. This helps to explain the passion with which agents subsequently insisted on their stars' 'real' dimensions: bust, waist and hip measurements became necessary for proper appreciation of the picture, just as the scale reference on a headquarters map enabled it to be read and interpreted by a military user. Marilyn's body, which the Seventh Division doctors said they would most like to *examine* yet which no one claimed from the morgue, reminds one of that penetrating gaze of the surgeon or cameraman which came into its own in the First World War. 'The painter,' writes Benjamin,

maintains in his work a natural distance from reality, the cameraman penetrates deeply into its web. There is a tremendous difference between the pictures they obtain. That of the painter is a total one, that of the cameraman consists of multiple fragments which are assembled under a new law.[22]

Like aerial reconnaissance photography, whose reading depends on everything that can be drawn from the rationalized act of interpretation, the use of endoscopy or scanners allows hidden organs to surface in an instrumental collage, an utterly obscene reading of the ravages of a trauma or a disease. This capacity to make the invisible visible – in the endless study of a picture to find significance in what appears to be a chaos of meaningless forms, or in that visual ease of examining film by hand which, according to Painlevé, roots cinema in scientific discovery – links up with the ways in which an army officer studies the enemy landscape, assesses the damage done to mostly camouflaged positions (trenches, encampments, bunkers), 'performing with observed procedures those unknown procedures that cinematic technique likes to summon forth' (Germaine Dulac).

The cinema industry made no mistake with its publicity. Once the star had been named 'body' and her picture painted on bombs and bombers, this body with no stable dimensions would soon be offered up in 'fragments' to the audience, in a repetition of the heterogeneous perception of the military voyeur. From Jean Harlow to Jane Russell, Lana Turner or Betty Grable, attention was drawn to a blown-up detail – legs, eyes, bottom, or whatever. The cinematic 'exposure' of external forms took over from the écorché of the old anatomy.

Griffith readily assimilated the futurist lessons of *Cabiria* for his own *Intolerance*: the blurring of temporal elements, improvisation without prior cutting, mobility of the camera, extensive use of montage to join in a relation of simultaneity actions taking place in ten different places and four different centuries, and so on. But, as we have seen, he experienced a new and 'intolerable' technological surprise on the military–industrial battlefield. This time it was the civilian camera which, despite the recentness of its invention, appeared prehistoric beside the lightning advance of the military tracking shot. Griffith's great period came to an end shortly after the war, in 1922 or thereabouts.

Abel Gance – a great admirer of Griffith, who was his elder by fourteen years – had also worked for the army during the First World War. He began his *J'Accuse* in 1917 when the rank-and-file troops were mutinying at the front, and many of his extras were wounded soldiers who were convalescing or had been invalided out (one of these was Blaise Cendrars). Gance's definition of the cinema was close to that of the 'war machine' with its fatal autonomy: 'Magical, spell-binding, capable of giving to the audience, in every fraction of a second, that strange sensation of four-dimensional omnipresence cancelling time and space.'

War is cinema and cinema is war, but in fact Gance did not yet realize the provisional character of this amalgam as far as the cinema was concerned. His numerous inventions (the triple screen – patented on 20 August 1926 – sound perspective, polyvision, magirama, etc.) give the sense of a tragic race after the all-pervasive dynamism of the military, a knock-on from their visual and acoustic techniques. The premature decline of Gance's work spelt the end of the race, the certainty that to overtake was now materially impossible, the defeat of a civilian cinematic power which 'had been incapable of inventing its own atomic bomb'.[23]

From now on the cinema would be no more than a bastardized form, a poor relation of military–industrial society. The art film, which had seemed an avant-garde of cinema, passed away of its own accord.

In 1905 Einstein enunciated his theory of energy and ten years later, in the midst of world war, he published his general theory of relativity. Giuseppe Peano, Haussdorf and von Koch made contributions to mathematical logistics and ideography; Kurt Gödel mathematically proved the existence of an object without producing it, his *existential proof* becoming, together with von Neumann's work and the famous *game theory*, the basis for contemporary nuclear strategy. Deviating from shapes and representations of physical reality, the scientific theory that underpinned the military effect also reached in half a century the surrealist heights of unknown cinematic territory, where the old fields of perception were completely destroyed.

While Hollywood, after the First World War, took to the most extravagant camera movements, Eisenstein in the Soviet Union talked of the series of engine combustions that drove a film forward. In his view, 'the concept of collision or conflict is the expression of Marxist dialectics in art.' Here too there were variations in the frame, fades and divided images, unexpected camera movements, back-tracking, sudden and unexplained intrusion of objects, characters and places, huge crowd movements.[24] As with Marinetti, the revelation of depth became strictly apocalyptic, since it aimed at dynamically 'finishing off' the dimensions of the world: 'As creators,' wrote the German architect Mendelsohn, 'we know how diversely the motor forces, the play of tensions, actually work at a detailed level.'[25]

Distance, depth, three-dimensionality – in just a few years of war, space became a training-ground for the dynamic offensive and for all the energies it harnessed. And since 'the harsh accents of its forward motion impel us towards a new clarity, the metallic roar of its matter plunges us into a new light', cinema became the metaphor for this object-shaping geometry, this fusion/confusion of genres which prefigured the terrifying species-mutation of later years, and for the exorbitant priority accorded to speed of penetration by war and the war industry which, after 1919, converted to producing means of communication and transport and commercializing air space.

It was not long before a mass industry, basing itself upon psychotropic

derangement and chronological disturbance, was directly applying cinematic acceleration to the realism of the world. This new cinema was particularly aimed at the ever wider public which had been torn from its
sedentary existence and marked down for military mobilization, exile and
emigration, proletarianization in the new industrial metropolises . . . and
revolution. War had everyone on the move, even the dead. Following the
success of the cabs which carried troops to the Marne battlefield in 1914,
the taxi companies made a fortune by ferrying the corpses back to their
families.

This to-and-fro movement, which made everyone a passer-by, an alien
or a missing person, extended war's aphasia into peacetime. In 1848, in
his famous *Principles of Political Economy*, John Stuart Mill had written
that 'to produce is to move'. But after 1914, the cinema became such a
powerful industry because now *to move was to produce*. (For his part,
Alain thought that 'superstition is to believe that one can move things.')

At the time few means of persuasion were available to the various
states. Newspapers could only reach a limited number of readers – one of
the largest, the *Daily Mail*, having a circulation of barely a million. Public
rallies were frequently held, but they too had a restricted impact since
political leaders could only address the crowd through short-range megaphones. This lack of propaganda instruments partly accounts for the air of
conspiracy that surrounded cinema technique: a kind of industrial prag-
matism, born out of intensive production of war pictures, generated films
which were the work of organized groups rather than a single author, so
that the old 'nickel odeon' soon became a nationalized activity, as in
Lenin's Russia. But it is often forgotten today that, after the separation of
Church and State in France, the fall of the divine-right monarchies and
empires all over Europe provided a unique historical opportunity for
cinema in the early part of the twentieth century.

The First World War brought an end to the privileged relations between
old religions and young military–industrial states. These states, founded
as in the Soviet Union upon overt violence, needed to create a new consen-
sus in order to be accepted by the greatest possible number (in order, that
is, to become legal) – hence the urgent necessity of imposing replacement
cults on the masses. The mystical, scientistic materialism of the nineteenth
century had, in assuming effective power, become a question of working
'miracles' of science by means of technology. Paradoxically, the supposed
advent of Reason in History became a cultural farrago, a technophile
syncretism, complete with a demonology and inquisitorial apparatus of
which the personality cult is one of the best-known aspects.

By the middle of the nineteenth century, recent scientific discoveries
and technological applications had unexpectedly brought mesmerism and
Swedenborgism back into fashion in Britain and the United States. It was

the hour of new illuminati, for whom 'the spirit' (God, the Eternal) was a magnetic fluid, an electrical phenomenon, kinetic heat. In 1845 the first spiritualist rappings were heard in the home of the Fox sisters in Hydesville. In the United States séances, dictations from beyond the grave, and other forms of hypnotic or medium-induced communication were used by individuals and religious sects 'to move back in time or across space without too much effort', as Polytechnic director Colonel de Rochas put it in 1900. The American Catholic Church itself did not completely disapprove of such goings-on. For it was a question of seeking out *new vectors of the Beyond*, after the provisional decline of the great religions and their loss of prestige to the state.

Meanwhile photography penetrated everywhere and in every milieu, even into the cloisters of Lisieux where the future saint Thérèse Martin had her convent retreat violated by the camera lens. This was the time when polemics began over the newly-discovered Shroud of Turin, the 'first photographic phenomenon in history', a veritable 'revelation' of photographic technique as a medium of iconolatry. Walter Benjamin quickly grasped and vigorously rejected the place that cinema could occupy within this mystical–scientistic structure, although he too was fascinated by the photographic aura. He saw that for many people (particularly in Germany, since a French invention was involved), 'photography remained a mysterious, disconcerting experience', with shadow and light which, as Jarry noted, could not easily penetrate each other.

This climate soon gave rise to a flourishing 'ghost industry' which used not only human but also photographic mediums. Since, for the new illuminati, ghosts were phenomena of electrical energy, why should they not also give off light and even be actually photogenic? After the Franco–Prussian War Leymarie, the editor of *Revue Spirite*, called on the professional assistance of Buguet to photograph the first ghosts – in reality, overexposures superimposed on images of 'the living' in such a way that they appeared among ordinary mortals as they passed through the darkroom. Leymarie was convicted of fraud and sentenced to a year in prison plus a fine of five hundred francs. Except when direct use was made of aura effects enhanced by skilful erasure, these ghosts were young and pretty models dressed in the pre-Raphaelite style. Given the high rates of mortality at that time, the customers who 'bought' the apparition were forging often tragic relations with the image itself.

As war was succeeded by epidemic, hitting especially hard the age-group between fifteen and thirty-five, the 'ghost industry' had a huge impact on the aesthetic and technical vocabulary of cinema. This was particularly striking in Germany, whose young cinema had only acquired artistic force during the war and which now counterposed supernatural dimensions to the crisis of natural dimensions revealed by the futurists and by the inordinate retribution of the Versailles Treaty.

Oskar Messter was one of the first to use twin projection to experiment with superimposition, and Stellan Rye – who died on the French front in 1914 – scored a major breakthrough for German cinema with his *Der Student von Prag*, the premonitory tale of a student who sells his reflected mirror-image to a wizard.[26] This image begins to act in the student's place, 'dishonouring' him and forcing him to remain a war-fixated conqueror. The student shoots at this irksome double in the hope of destroying it, but it is he who dies as a result. Noël Simsolo has written of this film: 'It is perhaps the first film which speaks of cinema. A person's picture, framed like a cinema-image, is stolen . . . the actor is responsible for the deeds that his image performs in accordance with another's wishes – director or wizard.'[27] Simsolo goes on to remind us that the two scriptwriters, Hans-Heinz Ewers and the great actor Paul Wegener, later worked on Nazi propaganda films during the Third Reich.

In cinema there is no longer such a thing as an 'accurate' reflection. 'Everything', Wegener said in 1916, 'depends on *a certain flow in which the fantastic world of the past rejoins the world of the present.*' The chaos of a non-sensory order installed itself alongside the quite visible order of the senses. Delirious new ghostly images, having been stolen, touched up and invoked anew, could be taken and sold as the enthralling object of a profitable trade in appearances, or could be projected in every direction in time and space. 'Already,' Duhamel remarked around 1930, 'I can no longer think what I like. *Moving images substitute themselves for my own thoughts.*' Cinema is war because, as Dr Gustave Le Bon wrote in 1916,

> War touches not only the material life but also the thinking of nations . . . and here we meet again the basic notion that it is not the rational which manages the world but forces of affective, mystical or collective origin which guide men. The seductive promptings of these mystical formulas are all the more powerful in that they remain rather ill defined . . . immaterial forces are the true steerers of combat.[28]

In the United States the first film actors had no surname or even christian name, but when the papers reported the death of the 'Biograph Girl' in 1910 this anonymity disappeared. The girl was finally identified as Florence Lawrence, and by a miracle she happened to be in the best of health. The announcement of her death, rather like those terrorist actions referred to in chapter one, had been no more than a publicity stunt. It is significant that the star system only really triumphed after 1914 in the new cinema industry, at a time when optical illusion became confused not just with the illusion of life but with the illusion of survival.

1. Anonymous photograph of spirit with superimposition. Late nineteenth century.

2. British soldiers in the trenches in 1917. 'In so far as the battlefield presented itself to the bare eyesight of men, it had no entirety, no length, no breadth, no depth, no size, no shape, and was made up of nothing.... In such conditions, each separate gathering of English soldiery went on fighting its own little battle in happy and advantageous ignorance of the general state of the action; nay, even very often in ignorance of the fact that any great conflict was raging' (Alexander Kinglake).

3. D.W. Griffith visiting the Somme trenches in early 1917. He was the only civilian film-maker authorized to make a propaganda film at the front, *Hearts of the World*. But he felt mortified that soldiers rarely saw the enemy in the battles that he wanted to film.

4. Gabriele d'Annunzio, Pastrone's co-scriptwriter on *Cabiria*, returning from an aerial mission in the First World War.

5. Camera mounted on a machine-gun emplacement, interfering with the aircraft's defences. The gun-grip is underneath the camera.

6. Mobile aerial-photography equipment. US Army, 1918.

7. Aerial photography and observation were the best sources of information in the First World War. A pilot is here commenting on a photo-mosaic of pictures taken during a mission.

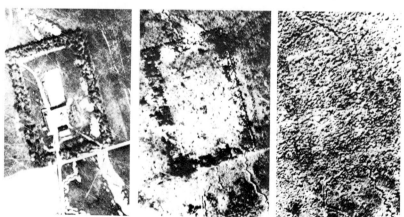

8. Montage of successive shots showing the destruction of a farm during the Great War. US Army.

9. Postcard game with a caricature of the Kaiser (1914–18).

10. In *Hell's Angels*, produced and directed by Howard Hughes in 1927–30, Jean Harlow rewards the surviving aviator.

11. Jean Painlevé shooting a 'cinemacrophotography' film in 1930.

12. Captain A.W. Stevens shooting a film for the US Air Force in 1929.

13. The emblem of Twentieth Century Fox. The play of light assumed growing importance after the First World War.

14. Plan for a triple-screen monumental cinema designed by the Spanish architect Fernandez Shaw in 1930, five years before Albert Speer's Nuremberg display. Evidently it was to be a drive-in cinema for cars and aeroplanes.

15. Howard Hughes arriving at Le Bourget airport during his flight round the world in 1938.

16. Major Goddard displaying USAF photographic material on 9 June 1939. In the background is a B-18 aircraft.

17. Adolf Hitler rehearsing sign-language for a public speech.

18. Advertisement in the magazine *Signal*, 1941.

19. British advertisement for air-raid shelters, 1941.

20. Cosmetics advertisement used as camouflage for British coastal defences, 1940.

21. German searchlight from World War Two.

22. Londoners sheltering in an Underground tunnel.

3

Abandon All Hope, Ye Who Enter
the Hell of Images *

In the final version of Gance's *J'Accuse*, the dead soldiers rise up before
Douaumont's illuminated charnel house and march past the living like so
many terrifying holograms.

After 1914, while old Europe was being covered with cenotaphs, in-
destructible mausoleums and other monuments to the glory of its dead
millions, the Americans, who had suffered fewer losses, were building
their great cinema temples – deconsecrated sanctuaries in which, as Paul
Morand put it, the public sensed the end of the world in an ambience of
profanation and black masses. A number of studies have recently been
made of this wave of cinema palaces which spread throughout the world
and finally came to an end around 1960. Their abrupt disappearance
clearly shows their historical necessity in the period between two wars
which, in reality, were but one conflict interrupted by a kind of twenty-
year armistice.

These monuments, of which little is now left but photographs,[1] seem
less unreal if one thinks back to those department stores which, a century
earlier, had infatuated the public as soon as they opened their doors in the
big cities of the West. The architectural vocabulary of the American
cinema cathedrals was already there in the agglomeration of heterogeneous styles, the huge naves and long gangways, the disproportionate
central staircase, and above all the imposing technological environment of
electricity, lifts, air conditioning, and so on. Mere commercial logic
seemed to go by the board, for the invention of marketing had the result
that *the whole commodity system of the young industrial civilization
henceforth presented itself within immaterial fields of perception.* When

---

*Abel Gance

Aristide Boucicaut thought up the 'mois du blanc'[2] one Boxing Day, he had just noticed that his department store was empty and that it was snowing outside. The idea, launched with a great fanfare, attracted a large number of customers who were determined to brave the weather simply because Boucicaut had elevated his merchandise to one of 'those precise, naked appearances in the mind' which 'the understanding lays up (with names commonly annexed to them) as the standards to rank real existence into sorts.'[3]

Not many years ago, some women spent most of their time in these monuments, as others would do in railway stations or in cinemas with continuous performances. Cinemas took over both from the department stores and from music halls. Nineteenth-century Europeans, observed Taine, were forever on the move to *see* new commodities; now, with the coming of the cinema, pure visions were for sale. The cinema became the major site for a *trade in dematerialization,* a new industrial market which no longer produced matter but light, as the luminosity of those vast stained-glass windows of old was suddenly concentrated into the screen.

'Death is just a big show in itself', said Samuel Lionel Rothapfel, son of a German shoemaker, one-time marine and inventor of the first cinema to be baptised a cathedral, the Roxy.[4] In other words, the speed effects of light created another form of collective memory in these new temples, an astronomical introversion comparable to that described by Evry Shatzmann: 'If you consider that observation takes place by means of light, which is propagated at a finite speed, things are observed in a past as far back as they are spatially distant.'[5]

There is a kind of cinematic 'heroization' in which the 'tragic lyricism of ubiquitousness and ever-present speed' renews the mythical chronos of aboriginality, that eternal present of native-born offspring for whom time is ceaselessly annulled in the irrevocable return of the end to the origin.[6] One thinks here of statements such as the following one made by Isser Harel, chief of Mossad:

After the creation of the Jewish state in May 1948, the search for Eichmann was one of the main objectives of the Israeli State Services because he was responsible for the fate of our six million dead . . . this was all the more imperative in that the Nuremberg trials, for reasons of foreign policy, had carefully avoided any talk of Jewish genocide: French, Poles, Hungarians, etc. had been exterminated in the concentration camps, but nowhere was it mentioned that a great majority of them were Jews. . . . Later, particularly with Professor Faurisson and his followers, the *reality* of the holocaust was also denied.

If Isser Harel's statement is taken literally, it says everything: the new aboriginality of the Jewish people rests on the existence in memory of six million missing persons who have to be made to reappear somewhere. The search for Eichmann was a priority because he had been not so much the butcher as the punctilious accountant of the holocaust, the functionary who 'called the victims by their right name'. The blindness of Nuremberg was a greater threat to the political existence of the State of Israel than any military violation of its frontiers.

In fact Faurisson and his kind built in a most disturbing way upon the work of disinformation that the Nazis had themselves undertaken forty years before. As Walter Laqueur has shown, the Jews were in the grip of an information implosion which prevented them from understanding what was actually being done. They were the first not to believe in their extermination.[7]

The director Veit Harlan has shown that Goebbels was a past master at disinformation. One of his specialities was the spreading of contradictory rumours, including some which mentioned extermination but were coupled with 'transparent' source material in the shape of photographs designed to devalue precise reports. There was also the pretence of 'colonization in the East', with articles and films purporting to show the relocation of Jews as settlers. Although more than two million Jews had already been killed by 1942, the Jewish press in Palestine still found grounds for reassurance about the fate of the agricultural information centres in Poland and elsewhere, 'interpreting signs that no longer had any meaning' and dismissing detailed accounts because they were too terrifying.[8] And yet, the psychic anaesthesia which made Jews incapable of looking reality in the face was not a specifically Nazi method but an age-old military technique based on the simple idea that 'man can only take a certain amount of terror'. Twenty-five years earlier, this statement by the military theorist Charles Ardant du Picq had borne heavily on the psychology and handling of the rank-and-file soldiers who were decimated in the '14–18 war. To paraphrase Kipling, one might say that the concept of reality is always the first victim of war.

Burying-beetles are always busy at the foundation or re-establishment of military states. And if *memory is science itself* for those who make war, the memory in question is not like that of a popular culture based upon common experience: rather, it is a parallel memory, a paramnesia, a mislocation in time and space, an illusion of the *déjà vu*. The state's only original existence is as a visual hallucination akin to dreaming. As General MacArthur said: 'Great soldiers don't die, they fade away.' It is an ancient belief, for Sparta, the first military democracy, was already based upon what have been called 'inorganic individualities', upon a subtle shift in meaning between birth and reproduction such that the relationship among Spartans has been seen as one not so much of equality as of *fellowship*.[9] For their part, the Jews held the City-State to be *a travesty of birth, a field of death dressed up as life.* In Athens, every warrior who was killed had a reborn double: to die in war was art for art's sake, and invocations in the agony of death were sufficient unto themselves. Happy to be born of mother earth, happy to return. The city of Antiquity began by gathering the dead from beneath scattered domestic hearths and placing them together in great suburban necropolises. As it grew more arduous to arrange a meeting with the departed heroes, Hermes the Psychic Undertaker took charge of establishing contacts, restoring to the state its natural protectors. Hermes: the god of *herme*, of the big stone and particularly the stone enclosing the camera obscura of the tomb, the 'Attic stele which brings death itself before us in a living picture'.

A presence around tombstones, a light kept burning, a cult of heroes – these are near-universal beliefs and practices, to be found in Asia as well as the North. In Iran in 1979, Ayatollah Khomeini planned to proclaim the Islamic Republic in that vast South Teheran necropolis where the victims whom the city had mourned for the past year or more lay buried. At the funerals of IRA members, it is not the spouses and mothers but fellow-combatants in penitents' hoods who wear black. The heroes are those who, in losing their real features, present and yet unknown, escape the sense-memory of their family and close ones. The American Mormons (the Church of Jesus Christ of Latter-day Saints) have decided to carry out a census of eighteen billion persons, both dead and alive, with the aim of baptising them all. To this end they travel across Europe and the world, going from town to village and putting the smallest civil register on microfilm that is then stored in a 200-metre-deep atomic shelter in the Rocky Mountains, a necropolis where film takes the place of bodies for all eternity.

Even closer to home, when the new French socialist state was born in May 1981, one of the first acts of President François Mitterrand was to perform an ambivalent act of worship. Studiously turning his back on the festive Parisian crowd, Mitterrand preferred to become a film for millions of television viewers as he moved rose in hand through the corridors of the Panthéon. With the cameras lying in ambush, he passed from one burial-place to the next, from Jean Jaurès to Jean Moulin, so that the small screen became a means of screening what lay beyond the grave. Just as Mendès-France said that history was not chronological, so Mitterrand reminded us that communication techniques are not necessarily of the present day but can be quite ancient and turned to the past.

Abel Gance made no mistake when he wrote in 1927, just as he was finishing *Napoleon*: 'All legends, all mythology and all myths, all founders of religions and all religions themselves look forward to their *luminous resurrection*, and the heroes are jostling at our doors to enter.' He further noted: 'Here we are, wondrously flashed-back into the time of the

Egyptians. . . . The language of the images is not yet up-to-date, because *we are not yet made for them.* There is not yet enough respect, enough worship, for what they express.'[10]

When Gance wrote these lines about hieroglyphs, the tomb of Tutan-khamun had recently been discovered in the Valley of the Kings. The field-work and fabulous trove had received wide publicity, mainly through the coverage of the American reporter-photographer Burton. It is well known how influential the 'Egyptian style' was on cinema and on the furnishing, decoration and architecture of picture-houses, as well as on the screen presence of actors like Rudolph Valentino, a veritable double of the young pharaoh. More generally, however, the priceless funerary discovery reminds us that all art is like death, an inertia of the instant, and thus a *speed change in the order of time as it is lived.* If the Egyptians already pre-recorded their lives, 'as if they were to die tomorrow yet built as if they were to live eternally', this is because they realized, like Cleopatra found-ing the 'society of inimitable livers', that since everything was happening then and there, they were living days that could never be imitated. When Agnès Varda suggested that for the Impressionists light corresponded to a certain idea of happiness, she was doubtless thinking that they were among the last to put this intensity of the moment into their painting, so that sunlight became an expression of time in a reaction against the frozen artificiality of studio-lighting. The motor of the film-camera sprang into life shortly after the decline of the old pictorial art (easel painting, por-traiture as a business) because it involved the re-establishment of a late sun-cult. And when Gance said that 'cinema is putting a sun in every image', he was merely repeating three thousand years on the words of Akhenaton's song: 'The sun creates millions of appearances.'

Everything in this sunlit world is dedicated to speed. Even the tomb contains the instruments of dromology (sophisticated vehicles, chariots, vessels), and sovereign Death is represented holding a symbolic whip and bit tightly to his chest. The beyond does not interrupt the days of the pharaoh. The departure of the animating soul leaves the body motionless, but for Egyptian art the point is not to see the body still moving since *everything goes on moving.* Egyptian 'realism' is essentially a cinematic temptation. Arranging the tomb thus becomes a dromoscopic pleasure for its future occupant, just as being buried with his Cadillac was a matter of 'open-grave driving' for a rich American recently in the news. Quite understandably, the passenger-to-be devotes major material and techno-logical resources to this task, comparable to those with which one prepares for a distant conquest or an expedition into unknown territory. Pictorial representation itself is a dromoscopic sketch, systematically juxtaposing autonomous events, and the habitual 'two plus one' method is conceived as *a rhythm imposed on the human retina.* Animation is produced by what the Egyptians called 'luminous vitality' – an expression which shows how well they had mastered the anatomical problem of perception and the production of appearance, not as something given but as an active operation of the mind. Much later Seurat rediscovered this with his 'divisionism', while Kandinsky and film-makers like Gance saw that *the first task is to speak to the eyes*. In Egypt there was no symmetry but only equivalences: walls were walls of images, limestone strips painted from top to bottom on which figures passed 'in action'. Once more we are very close to the definition of chronophotography: 'Successive images representing the different positions that a living being with a certain gait has occupied in space at a given moment.'[11]

Such movement, which is actually a movement of withdrawal, plunges us directly into ethnology. Whereas the modern dreamer, as Jean Duvignaud has remarked,[12] represses his dreams and will not admit to them, in ancient societies revery and paradoxical sleep are cultivated as major activities and it is of their essence that one should be able to talk about them in words. 'Doing *kabary*' was the expression used by Malagasy shepherds at the foot of Mandraka. '*Rökut pit*' (absent sleep) is how the Jorai refer to someone who has fallen asleep, but '*rökut*' is also said of someone who is absent from his home, on a real journey by road. Stretched out on a mat *as if already dead*, the Jorai dreams because his *böngat* has gone off walking. It is this walk which provides the inert Jorai with his dream images, and with the tale that he will later tell, impossible to locate in geographical space or astronomical time.

These practices too are well-nigh universal. When the invention of printing revolutionized Renaissance Europe with its *silent reading*, the often religious paramnesia of the dream narrative (one thinks also of the birth of the novel, whose heroes are travellers en route in an unbounded universe) no longer involved spoken exchanges in human gatherings but rather industrial reproduction of a standard text. Millions of books were published within a few decades, prefiguring the later spread of photography, cinema and now electronics. The innovation of silent reading had the effect that everyone believed what they read, for at the moment of reading they had the illusion that they were alone in seeing it, just as the inert dreamer created an equivalence between the waking state and paradoxical sleep. Numerous affinities exist between the instantaneities of writing and photography, both being inserted in time which is 'exposed' rather than simply passing. Printing already introduces a new technological interface: the means of communication slow and retain the immediate, fixing it in an exposure time that escapes daily wear and the calendar of society, opening a gap between the instrument of transmission and our capacity to assume present existence. If we give a new book to two children, the enjoyment will always be compromised for the one who reads it second. The metro passenger reading a paper over his neighbour's shoulder puts him in a similar position, for although tens of thousands of other people are also reading the paper at that moment it is annoying to have to share it with someone else. *Pace* Robespierre, history is not read as a past charged with 'non-presence'; the very fact of its mediated transmission implies a journey through empty and soon heterogeneous time (Benjamin).

A false equation of sign-reading with knowledge, and even with the whole of knowledge, gave rise to the imperialism of the fourth estate – the power, that is, of press and communications media directly involved in the atypical temporality of broadcasting technology. When the press speaks of its own 'objectivity', it can easily make one believe in its truthfulness. For the newspaper's present superiority over a book is that it has no author, the reader taking it in as a truth that he alone knows, true because he 'believes his eyes'. We can see why journalists with their anonymous style have acquired such immense power in every field of publishing, as well as in politics at the crossroads of the media. In France the old *presse d'opinion* vanished after 1914, along with its great polemicists and writer-reporters – men like Dumas, London or Kipling for whom the novel was truly 'a mirror walking on the highway' (Stendhal). It is evident that the long-range media have gradually taken over from the 'anima', and that the motor (twin projector, both producing speed and propagating images) now recounts the journey and supplies the dream images. Like the motor-car, which ensures 'that the traveller's head bursts under the pressure of a mass of truncated images vainly striving to join up with each other',[13] the thresholds of dynamic transformation trigger the dissipation of visual structures. It has been written of Eisenstein's and Alexandrov's *October* (1927):

> The inner tension of the film, the inner current of the montage, set up such strong disturbances that no logical determination seems tenable any more . . . with no anchorage in space and time, the readability of the shapes is called into question by such a large number of shots that it is impossible to hold them in memory.[14]

The technology of mixing, generalized to this degree, actually achieves that 'still moving' which ethnology found on the mat of the inert dreamer. It can thus easily appear as a substitute religion, as Jean-Jacques Servan-Schreiber unwittingly suggests in his recent book *Le Nouveau Défi*, which is more an act of faith or Pascalian wager than a perspective with anything remotely rational to it. One can only wonder at this immaterial logistical pantheism, in which social well-being rests upon advanced technologies that bear no relationship to reality. The exposure time of silent reading vanishes in the anatomical eye of the camera, releasing a flood of illiteracy in the developed countries. Electronic games have transformed the 'softening up' effects of wonder and astonishment of earlier cultures, since now it is more a question of seeing than of understanding. Similarly, the mass of viewers have become less interested in team games like cycling or football than in live broadcasts of sports like tennis, where a little ball bounces unpredictably for hours across a court much as a computer-player pilots synthetic blobs back and forth on an electronic screen.

Paul Claudel, referring to the stained-glass windows of old cathedrals, once said: 'All those colours together, all those various points, all that does not remain motionless.' In the thirteenth century, Guillaume Durrand wrote of the technically innovative Chartres windows: 'The stained-glass is divine writing which pours the *brightness of the real sun* (that is, of God) into the church (that is, into the hearts of men) whilst iluminating them.' Everything visible appears to us in the light, we believe our eyes and the light calmly appears to us as *the truth of the world*. The early-twentieth-century comparison of giant cinemas to cathedrals was based on the fact that the latter were already solar projection rooms, which took root in society with the same lightning speed. Their demolition began in similar manner, long before the French Revolution, in that late-seventeenth-century 'illuminism' of the Enlightenment which prefigured the scientism of the nineteenth century. We should not forget that, ever since Antiquity, the liturgy was a *public service* which combined the logistical organization of distant expeditions, religious ceremonies laid down by the spiritual authorities, and spectacles conceived as 'special effects' (*deus ex machina*). To paraphrase Heidegger, we might say that in the cathedral Christ is already dead, since the new sanctuary aspires to expose science, at once and in its entirety, to the power of the world, without troubling to mix in the disciplines of human existence (nation, customs, state, war, poetry, thought, belief, disease, madness, death, technology). Before it became the throne of totality, the Christian sanctuary was a stronghold, a bunker, a fortified church for those who remained within it; all their powers and capacities were deployed and strengthened *in, through and as combat*. It is often said to be difficult or impossible to imagine the attitude of medieval Christians in their new churches. But already today, we can no longer precisely imagine how film-goers of the thirties or even fifties behaved as they streamed towards the cinema-cathedrals of the military state.

'World War One was the reason for Hollywood', said Anita Loos.[15] The cinema-town (Cinecittà, Hollywood . . .) of the military–industrial era succeeded the theatre-town of the ancient City-State. At first, studios and cinemas were built in the suburbs like the necropolises of old. This was because in practice theatre still held *droit de cité* as the fount of living relations, whereas the silent cinema was reserved for an unintegrated (often unnaturalized) migrant proletariat sprawling illiterate in the limbo-like outskirts.

The cinema trance, like that of the combatant, rested upon a certain kind of social suffering, the daily grind to which life was reduced in over-populated suburbs where East met West without merging in civic fellow-ship. In whatever way, the target population was that 'shapeless sociological conglomerate' of the military–industrial proletariat, which was calmly summoned to factory and battlefield at a time when the 'Bolshevik threat' stretched from Munich to the gates of India and when the Americans expected to wake up every day with the Russians camped in Paris.

Paradoxically, the cinema gratified the wish of migrant workers for a lasting and even eternal homeland, giving them a new kind of freedom of the city. For the religion of ceramics cinematography substituted recorded film, a standardized Valhalla with its images of various types of event, object and character. The cinema auditorium would not be a new city agora for the living where immigrants from the whole world might gather and communicate with one another; it was much more of a cenotaph, and the essential capacity of cinema in its huge temples was to shape society by putting order into visual chaos. This made cinema the black mass neces-sary for the country to achieve a new aboriginality in the midst of demo-graphic anarchy. In his memoirs Marcel Pagnol emphasizes this unfailing penetrativeness of the cinema beam:

> A theatre audience of a thousand cannot all sit in the same place, and so one can say that none of them sees the same play. In order to reach his audience in the right way, a dramatist has to take his duck-gun and stuff it with a thousand pieces of shot so that one pull of the trigger will hit a thousand different targets. Cinema solves this problem, however, because what each member of the audience sees from anywhere in the room (or in a country, where there is an audience of millions) is the exact picture taken by the camera. If Charlie Chaplin looks at the lens, his picture will look straight at anyone who sees it, whether they are on the left or the right, upstairs or downstairs. . . . So there is not just an audience of a thousand (or millions if all the cinemas are included); *now there is only one audience which sees and hears exactly as the camera and microphone do.*[16]

According to J.F.C. Fuller, any individual, man or woman, is poten-tially a nervous target, and in fact it was the precision of the camera-shot which first created audience panic at the Lumières' 'motion demon-strations' of the train's arrival at la Ciotat, when everyone felt that they risked being crushed or injured by the train. This kind of fear, akin to the sense of speed that people seek on roller coasters, did not disappear but simply became more pernicious as the audience learnt to control its nervous reactions and began to find death amusing. In Westerns, death had to become more and more common, and the body count started – just as in those army headquarters where a high number of casualties and a depletion of men and matériel were considered to be marks of a commander's talent or personality, even proofs of the orthodox nature of his art. Moreover, the duel of the homicide–suicide couple (hetero or homo) which is the core of war's vagaries is endlessly reproduced and chewed over by the military–industrial cinema, becoming such a powerful model that it rapidly overturns age-old customs. The sociologist Lewis Feuer has pointed out that the emotional overload in the Western has completely changed people's mentality in Asia, where the ritual of classical drama most often had the 'goodies' suffering at the hands of victorious 'baddies'. Now a new philosophy of history has established itself in the East with the notion of 'just war'.[17]

At the time when Wells was writing *The Time Machine*, 'Hale's Tour' was already setting the audience up as aggressors in a room ten foot deep with seats on either side of a central aisle, just as in a railway carriage travelling at top speed. The film itself, taken from behind or in front of a locomotive crossing varied countryside, was projected onto a screen at the end of the room which served as a kind of windscreen. The whole performance was usually financed by transport or arms companies, which were to lose no time in distinguishing themselves during the First World War.

Shortly afterwards, V. Bush noticed that young people in their thousands, without suspecting a thing, were becoming involved in veritable military training camps simply through their passion for cars and motorcycles, mechanics and wirelesses, and that if the time came, such training could very rapidly be converted into an aptitude for building the complex apparatus of war. Cinemas, too, were training camps which bonded people together in the face of death agony, teaching them to master the fear of what they did not know – or rather, as Hitchcock put it, of what did not exist. 'In essence,' he once said, 'we create violence out of our memories and not out of what is directly presented to our vision, just as in childhood the viewer himself fills the blanks and his own head with pictures that he manufactures a posteriori.'[18]

The essayist John A. Kouwenhoven, in a work on 'what is American in America', later asked which common factor could bind together such 'symptoms' as skyscrapers, chewing-gum, assembly-lines, cartoon strips, baseball, and so on. In fact, the military–industrial cinema took up this heap of signs and information to compound not only the unity of the nation but the personality profile of each new citizen. In the Second World

War, Allied counter-espionage used questionnaires probing such seemingly disparate characteristics in order to unmask Nazi fifth-columnists
who had infiltrated Britain or the United States. And GIs in Europe always
found the same collection of symptoms (bible, chewing-gum, toilet paper,
etc.) in their packs. This tradition was continued after the war with the
famous Liberty ships, but it was both a strength and a weakness because,
once perception was deprived of such logistical support, the army proved
incapable of facing a difficult campaign, as in North Africa in 1942–44 or
in Korea and later Vietnam.

The star system, after 1914, used these same types of trigger, which
'oscillated in zones higher than the universe of practical things and lower
than the disembodied forces that animate such things' (Arnheim). At the
very beginning, the big US corporations and film directors had been
violently opposed to a theatre-type star system in the cinema, and when
actors were finally accepted by name they were regarded as so many
'fellow-creatures'. Losing their real traits in the manner of ancient heroes,
slipping from the immediate memory of their family and friends, they
became inorganic individuals through an arbitrary selection of indefinitely
reproducible common features. Soon, even in their private lives, they were
not supposed to stray from the paramnesiac placement that was written
into their contract. Ingrid Bergman's illegitimate pregnancy (she, the
young Joan of Arc!) and her relationship with Rossellini led to her being
questioned by the US Senate at the time of the Korean War, and subsequently ruined her Hollywood career.

Cinema begins at its palace arches where letters of fire blazon forth the
names of its stars. It is like 'life's splendour' which, according to Kafka,
'forever lies in wait about each one of us in all its fullness, but veiled from
view, deep down, invisible, far off. If you summon it by the right word, by
its right name, it will come. This is the essence of magic, which one does
not create but summons.'[19] As part of the isolating world of indirect
perception, the star is an iconic figure which cannot be compared to the
flesh-and-blood presence of theatrical creation. Vestal virgin of that 'sun
in each image' (Gance), guardian of a national hearth of incomparable
brightness, the star suffers a fate like that of the ancient priestess: to give
in to mortal love and all-too-human passions spells the end of her own
immortality, the beginning of an immurement diligently organized by the
censors, politicians or puritanical leagues. In fact, as soon as the cinema's
civic potential became evident after 1914, it was placed under house arrest
and brought under a system of regulation based on the methods of
wartime black propaganda.

False rumours, belated revelations, trading on personality, banning
orders, trials, denunciations, inquisitions, witch-hunts – in all this, dread
of the Communist or Nazi enemy was mixed up with the terror of drugs

and the prohibition of alcohol and sex. In the United States Will Hays, a former member of the Harding administration, was solicited by the producers themselves to take charge of film censorship in the twenties. The civic, religious and family leagues were joined by police chiefs, army officers, the Hearst press, anti-drug agents, and so on. Even after the black-lists and the tragedy of McCarthyism, a 1975 report of the Trilateral Commission was still denouncing 'artists and intellectuals' as marginal, irrecuperable elements. At the same time, however, the report called for compulsory curbs on world economic growth and announced that the democratic model based on the family cell, in which many Americans still believed, was falling into disrepair. Hollywood had lost its reason for existence.

Here too one is struck by the similarity with the theatrical world, whose music-hall stars or divas ostensibly led 'immoral careers' as courtesans. Sarah Bernhardt, for example, went onto police records for prostitution – she who, paradoxically, helped to make Zukor's fortune by starring in *Queen Elizabeth*, which he bought from the British for 28,000 dollars and showed in New York on 12 July 1912 in a specially hired theatre, after a publicity campaign tending to suggest that the audience would be able to see the renowned Sarah in the flesh. Playing on the confusion between bodily presence and cinema, Al Lichtman went on to hire many more theatres to show the film. Zukor himself netted 80,000 dollars from this novel swindle and used the money to set himself up as a producer. Soon the producers would be writing into star contracts a clause that forced them to conceal their private lives in the manner recommended to leading politicians. Some, like Greta Garbo, who loved John Gilbert in front of the cameras, never lost their fear of any 'proxemic' look.[20]

The blazing of the female star, in a country where women, like Blacks, had long struggled for recognition of their civil rights, reminds us that at the foundation or restoration of a military state, in fusion with its intense burial activity, a whole series of exchanges and transfers of power take place between male warriors and logistical spouses[21] – that is to say, between natural reproduction of the old gynaecocracy (in which kinship is mostly matrilinear) and all the techniques for preserving and reproducing the new City-States, from the fortress designed as Mother through the industrial die of the weaponry to the military–industrial cinema itself. The ethnological evidence is always there, and always the same. In Europe, such exchanges resumed with the establishment of feudalism, particularly with the Salic law in France, Spain and elsewhere.

At that time, women played an ambiguous role in narratives, emanating from a rather uncertain and dangerous world of water and impenetrable, magical forest. Male partners, when found, had strayed into an unfamiliar environment where women were at ease and in a sense the mistresses. Already in Jorai legend woman is the fairy-hunter, the one who organizes the lures, weaves and places the nets into which game and enemies will fall. And yet, the Jorai woman does not herself take part in hunting or warfare, leaving the role of final killer to the male. When Europe's strategic fortresses were being built, woman still kept her power as tactician and an old Norman dictum stated that 'there is no fortress where a woman has not first set hand or foot.' One thinks of Vivian, or the Mélusine of the House of Lusignan, a fairy–woman–animal who cast her protective stronghold over a territory grown huge through her topological wiles, or of that other enchantress who was found in the woods by a knight and agreed to stay with him on condition that she never heard him utter the word 'death'. Those 'precise, naked appearances' which John Locke discussed in connection with abstraction are found again here as models coming from no one knows where.

In the courtly novel, the woman's body soon merges completely with the stronghold and its snares. She herself is seen as a 'box full of surprises and strategems' which can make the duel of heterosexual love and war last indiscriminately for ever.

As the colonial City of Antiquity promiscuously adopted the gods of conquered or neighbouring peoples, so did Hollywood in its heyday drain and adapt the talents of the Western world, in a ceaseless quest for the abstract yet visually perceptible models required to programme the common features of a universal star system. In her brief career Louise Brooks, the *femme fatale* Lulu in Pabst's *Die Büsche der Pandora* (1928) and described by Lotte Eisner as that 'uncommon earthly creature endowed with animal beauty', was one of the distant mediums of the fairy-woman and the immortal Pandora. Herself created by Hephaistos, the god of fire and forges, Pandora kept the fateful box containing both human happiness and unhappiness – a box at the bottom of which remained nothing but hope.

At the end of the Middle Ages, that Hollywood favourite Joan of Arc had already crystallized these universal symptoms, her great power deriving from her capacity to alter the course of a hundred years' war. Originally a shepherdess living in the woods and meadows, she was accepted as a strategist with an ease which, though surprising today, was ethnologically quite conceivable in those days. At the age of seventeen, then, she was entrusted with an army and had princes under her command. But she went unarmed into combat and, like the Jorai women, did not participate in the male carnage, taking great care over her transsexual appearance and sublimating her warrior's equipment (armour, horse, standard) as instruments of recognition. In this way, she powerfully intervened in the conduct of battles, those circumstantial fields of perception which have always been the main arenas for the fast-stimulating slogans and emblems later employed in commercial design and the film industry.

Joan's fate was exactly like that of the female logistician of ancient times. After the army-state was re-established in Rheims, she was sold, tried and sent to the stake as a witch, a fairy-woman specially for the occasion, and this is still how she appears in Shakespeare's work. The Maid of Orleans or Artemis of Antiquity brings us back to sexual abstinence and the uniformity of a chaste model. And it was precisely these grounds of resemblance which brought on Ingrid Bergman's downfall in 1949, when she became illegitimately pregnant a year after filming *Joan of Arc.*

After the Civil War and the conquest of the West, the Americans began to put on stage and to direct the 'true heroes' of the barely pacified South or Far West: Calamity Jane, Buffalo Bill, Sitting Bull, and so forth. After the 1914–18 war and again during the 'Cold War', large numbers of ex-combatants relived their exploits in front of the camera and some, like Audie Murphy, managed to use their military titles and decorations to make a film career for themselves. When a Hollywood old-timer finally canvassed for the presidency of the United States, he had the idea of putting on a TV spectacular, a strange military-cum-political festival in which genuine veterans of the war like General Bradley rubbed shoulders with Hollywood survivors, sundry imitators and politicians' doubles. Ronald Reagan himself, seated on a throne, presided with his wife over hallucinatory games worthy of Lewis Carroll or Monty Python.

After his election in January 1982, Reagan asked his friend Charles Wick, a California millionaire and director of *Voice of America*, to organize 'the greatest show since the creation of the world'. The stars were to be a dozen heads of state and government, each of whom had to read a message expressing their country's solidarity with the Polish people and their opposition to the Soviet-backed regime of General Jaruzelski. These somewhat austere communications were lightened by the presence of singers, musicians and actors like Frank Sinatra, Charlton Heston, Kirk Douglas and Bob Hope, and the whole show was broadcast by satellite across the United States and the world in a 'weekend of solidarity' organized by Westerners. The North American side of the operation, however, posed serious problems as *Voice of America* is a long-standing propaganda agency which does not have the right to broadcast to the United States itself. Nevertheless, Congress saw fit to give its approval and the show went ahead.

In March 1983 President Reagan signed 'National Security Directive 75' which, though not published, has been substantively quoted in the *Los*

Angeles Times. Its author, Richard Pipes, is a former adviser on the USSR for the National Security Council. Among other things, this directive outlined the so-called 'Project Democracy' – in reality, an appeal for greater propaganda efforts to accompany US economic sanctions and rearmament. The administration accordingly asked for a credit of 85 million dollars in films, books and means of communication to promote democracy in general and free trade unions in particular, the manna to be distributed mainly in Western and Eastern Europe. Once again, Congress did not fail to release major resources, which were soon swept up.[22]

In 1982 the Soviet news agency TASS characterized the 'Let Poland Be Poland' operation as a provocative act of telesubversion instigated by the White House. Brushing aside any challenge, President Ronald Reagan had carried with him to the awesome pinnacle of global power an old stock of perceptual material that faithfully reproduced the scenes and methods of Hollywood's past. As a B-movie actor, Reagan had testified for the prosecution at the sessions of the House Committee on Un-American Activities which preceded the notorious trial of the 'Hollywood Ten', and at the height of McCarthyism he had been chairman of the Actors' Guild. 'Directive 75', then, was a way of drawing on his cinema knowledge to prepare a new kind of frontier violation, a new and logistically powerful audiovisual force which, alongside the Euromissiles, would more closely integrate the European suburb into America's system of security. It was conceived as an indispensable complement to 'power projection', in a year when Weinberger's budgetary report was laying stress on the geographical exposure of states in the modern world.

With this deneutralization of the East–West media, we are clearly heading towards a new Yalta and perhaps towards a new world state. In the last century Ratzel defined war as the taking of one's frontiers to another's territory, and there can be no doubt that the world-wide Reagan Show involved an attempt to go beyond the ancient founding rites of the state. The actor-turned-president enjoyed bestowing on stars like Sinatra and Heston a status as immortal beings of the City, with a political power really capable of founding the American state and its cultural hold on the world. Still, the day after 'Let Poland Be Poland', a *Libération* journalist could report that 'the Reagan show did not draw a full house'. The 500,000-dollar spectacular, with its curious endgame atmosphere, had only limited success and the mass of dissatisfied TV viewers turned away from the stars of cinema and politics alike.

The journalist's expression was interesting because it compared the world to a single movie-house, as if 'the greatest show since the creation of the world' was at the same time the smallest. This brings us to that 'imposture of immediacy' denounced by the theologian Dietrich Bonhoeffer – at once a crisis of dimensions and a crisis of representation.

4

The Imposture of Immediacy*

Once the optical telegraph came into operation in 1794, the remotest battlefield could have an almost immediate impact on a country's internal life, turning upside down its social, political and economic field. The instantaneity of action over a distance was already an accomplished fact. Since then, as many people have noted, geographical space has been shrinking with every advance in speed, and strategic location has lost importance as ballistic systems have become more widespread and sophisticated. This technological development has carried us into a realm of factitious topology in which all the surfaces of the globe are directly present to one another.[1]

After the war of movement of mechanized forces, the time came for a strategy of Brownian movement, a geostrategic homogenization announced at the end of the last century in Mackinder's theory of the single 'World Island' into which various continents are supposedly contracting. (One is reminded of the war in the Malvinas, whose remoteness did not dampen the British ardour for Antarctic contraction.) With the great universal or colonial exhibitions, it was no longer necessary for people to travel to distant lands; the faraway could be presented to them as such, on the spot, in the form of more or less obsolescent scale models. The transport revolution made itself felt less in the desire for exoticism than in a new endogeny. In breaking open one's normal surroundings through a lightening trip to dreamlands, one could conjure away the trip and not even know one was travelling.

The Disney Corporation (which the French have consulted for the ghostly Universal Exhibition of 1989) took over the idea for Disneyland

---

*Dietrich Bonhoeffer

and then for EPCOT (the Experimental Prototype of the Community of Tomorrow). Walt Disney, speaking on 15 November 1965 at a memorable press conference held in the great lounge of Orlando's Cherry Plaza, described EPCOT as 'a new town of revolutionary design where we will try to solve *the communication and environmental problems posed for inhabitants of the cities of the future*'. Disney died suddenly thirteen months later, after the bulldozers had begun work on the eleven thousand hectares of Florida swampland purchased in 1964, an area larger than that of San Francisco.

It is significant that Disney's successors decided to solve the 'communication problems' of the city of the future by erecting the 'Showcase of the World'. Here past, present and future are telescoped together, and the five continents, represented by assorted visual relics of monuments and real objects, lie overlapping on the narrow shoreline of an artificial lake. The buildings and the perfectly copied cars and trains are a fifth of the normal size – a scaling down that Disney saw as the essence of *dream creation* – and 'cinema knowledge' here repeats the strategist's negation of dimensions.

When the offer of a trip 'Around the World in Eighty Minutes' shone in lights outside cinemas in the thirties, it was already clear that film was superimposing itself on a geostrategy which for a century or more had inexorably been leading to the direct substitution, and thus sooner or later the disintegration, of things and places. In 1926, in the Paramount 'Hall of Nations' in New York, Adolf Zukor had the idea of bringing under one roof a collection of representative material from ruins around the world, as if to assemble the last witnesses of a physical universe that had vanished into the special effects of communication machines. Rich Americans like John D. Rockefeller Jr followed this example by incorporating genuine pieces of architecture from medieval churches or castles into modern architectural structures, while the funerary handprints of stars left in the concrete sidewalk of Grauman's Chinese Theatre in Hollywood already prefigured the 'human negatives' of the atomic age.

Despite the massive accumulation of documents, publicity and films, young army recruits still say in response to questions that they cannot *imagine what a war would be like*. They are like that rookie in a fine chapter of Clausewitz's *On War* who, before facing the battlefield for the first time, looks at it from afar in astonishment and 'for a moment still thinks he is at a show'. The soldier then has to leave the calm of the surrounding countryside and to move ever closer to what might be regarded as the epicentre of battle, crossing one zone after another in which the intensity of danger continually increases. To the accompaniment of roaring cannons, whistling shells and quaking earth, more and more of his

comrades collapse around him, dead or suddenly maimed . . .'beneath
that steel storm in which the laws of nature appeared suspended, the mid-
winter air quivered as in the scorching days of summer and its flicker set
stationary objects dancing to and fro.'[2] Here the static sense of the world
has come to an incomprehensible end. 'Beyond a certain threshold,'
Clausewitz remarks, 'the light of reason moves in a different medium and
is reflected in a different manner.'[3] Once his customary faculties of perception and reasoning have let him down, the soldier has to display that military virtue which consists in believing that he will come through it all. To
be a survivor is to remain both actor and spectator of a living cinema, to
continue being the target of subliminal audiovisual bombardment or, in
the colloquial language of French soldiers, to 'light up' (*allumer*) the
enemy. It is also to try to postpone one's own death, that last technological accident or 'final separation of sound and image' (William Burroughs).

During the Second World War, while still a child, I experienced first-
hand the fierce flight of strategic bombing and, later, witnessed a series of
land battles in the company of a former artillery liaison officer, a survivor
from the '14–18 war who taught me how easily a tested mind could cut
through such a subliminal barrage, could locate and materialize in space
the atmospheric dimensions of a battle, and could anticipate what the
different parties intended to do. To cut a long story short, my old friend
jubilantly described the *scenario* of battle which I, being a newcomer, saw
only as its *special effects*. Young American GIs advancing to dangerous
battlefield positions used the most eloquent expression: 'We're off to the
movies.'

After 1945, this cinematic artifice of the war machine spread once more
into new forms of spectacle. War museums opened all over liberated
France at the sites of various landings and battles, many of them in old
forts or bunkers. The first rooms usually exhibited relics of the last
military–industrial conflict (outdated equipment, old uniforms and
medals, yellowing photographs), while others had collections of military
documents or screenings of period newsreels. It was not long, however,
before the invariably large number of visitors were shown into huge,
windowless rooms resembling a planetarium or a flight (or driving)
simulator. In these *war simulators*, the public was supposed to feel like
spectators–survivors of the recent battlefield. Standing in near-total darkness, they would see a distant, accurately curving coastline gradually light
up behind the vast pane of a panoramic windscreen, which then displayed
a rush of events indistinctly represented by dim flashes, rough silhouettes
of aircraft and motor vehicles, and the glimmer of fires. It was as if newsreels had been too 'realistic' to recapture the pressure of the abstract
surprise movements of modern war; and so, the old diorama method, with

its enhancement of the visual field, was brought into service to give people the illusion of being hurled into a virtually unlimited image. If one thinks of the cinema-mausoleums or atmospheric cinemas of the thirties, one can see in this a new outflanking of immediate reality by the cinematic paramnesia of the war machine. Shortly afterwards, in the 1950s, the grandson of the famous conjuror Robert Houdin invented the immediately popular 'Son et Lumière', a kind of open-air museum in which the past is reinjected into real places (temples, castles, landscapes) by means of projectors, sound equipment, artificial mist and, more recently, laser graphics. Similarly, in the American 'freedomlands' one can see 'Old Chicago' collapse and rise again from the flames every twenty minutes, or join in the Civil War and escape by the skin of one's teeth through the gunsmoke as the opposing sides open fire. Because of their overexposure in time, the material supports thus lose out to artificial lighting and become no more than a crepuscular threshold. The audience itself no longer knows whether the ruins are actually there, whether the landscape is not merely simulated in kaleidoscopic images of general destruction.

The sites chosen for museums of the Second World War remind us that these fortress-tombs, dungeons and bunkers are first and foremost camerae obscurae, that their hollowed windows, narrow apertures and loopholes are designed to light up the outside while leaving the inside in semi-darkness. In his pencil-like embrasure, the look-out and later the gunner realized long before the easel painter, the photographer or the film-maker how necessary is a preliminary sizing-up. 'You can see hell much better through a narrow vent than if you could take it in with both eyes at once', wrote Barbey d'Aurevilly, evoking the sort of squint necessary in taking aim and firing. This action, like the seductive wink so fashionable in the thirties, increased the depth of the visual field while reducing its compass. As recent experiments in anarthoscopic perception have shown,

> It is not enough to know that one is looking through a crack; it is also necessary to see the crack and in certain circumstances the observer may even invent it. In any case, it has been proved that the form of the aperture influences the perceptual identification of objects, and that visual tracking is a constitutive element in anarthoscopic perception of a moving shape.

More simply, the soldier's obscene gaze, on his surroundings and on the world, his art of hiding from sight in order to see, is not just an ominous voyeurism but from the first imposes a long-term patterning on the chaos of vision, one which prefigures the synoptic machinations of architecture and the cinema screen. In the act of focusing, with its proper angles, blind spots and exposure times, the line of sight already heralds the perspectival vanishing-line of the easel painter who, as in the case of Dürer or Leonardo, might also be a military engineer or an expert in siege warfare.

The nineteenth-century development of viewfinders precisely allowed the view to be 'found' and 'snapped' for military purposes, within interpretative codes for fixing the three-dimensional identity of two-dimensional images. This introduced a new reading of the battlefield, but also considerably increased the impotence and obscenity of the military decision-maker, now in ever greater danger of being tracked down and eliminated. Thus, in order to escape two-dimensional observation from anchored reconnaissance balloons four or five hundred metres up, the army began to bury its strongholds and outworks in a third dimension, throwing the enemy into a frenzy of interpretation. Invisible in its sunken depths, the camera obscura also became deaf and blind, its relations with the rest of the country now depending entirely on the logistics of perception, with its technology of subterranean, aerial and electrical communication. Already, what I have called the problem of the 'third window' – how to light the surrounding world without seeing it – posed itself in a most acute way.[4] From now on, strategy is concealed in the special effects of signals and communications:

> Located in deep shelters that open onto communication trenches, the projectors invented by General Mangin can send messages over a distance of more than eighty kilometres. The light from a powerful oil-lamp is concentrated in a telescope by means of a concave mirror. This telescope is fitted with a moveable shutter, so that one can obtain either a constant beam or a short burst or a long burst corresponding to the dot and dash of the Morse code (*Ecole du génie français*, 1887).

The inner walls of the central command posts became screens covered with gridded maps whose ceaseless animation abstractly logged the slightest movement of troops in what were still proximate theatres. About 1930, some countries, including Britain, wound down their conventional means of defence and concentrated on research into perception. This reorientation led to the development of cybernetics and radar, as well as advancing the sciences of goniometry, microphotography and, as we have seen, radio and telecommunications. Thus, during the Second World War, the military commands and war cabinets no longer needed to set up their bunkers near the field of battle, but were able to remain in Berlin or London, in command centres which bore a passable resemblance to huge theatre-halls, for a war which had already become a Space Opera.

No longer having any real extension in space, these centres of interaction received an endless mass of information and messages from the most scattered points and radiated it back into their own, defined universe. In a sense, they may be said to have taken over the inertia of the old *Kammerspiel*, with its subjection to the pressure of time. But in these aseptic chambers so overwhelming was the sense of *negative charge*, so bare the visual and acoustic representation, that Hitler decided to introduce sound effects into his control-room at Bruly-le-Pesch when he was planning Operation Sealion. For the miniaturization of technological power, reducing space and time to nothing, was incompatible with the expansive imagination of the Nazi *Lebensraum* and could only be countered with artificial depth and grandiosity.

5

The 'Fern Andra' Cinema

Jesse Lasky has recorded that when the United States finally went to war in 1916, everyone in Hollywood was gripped by patriotic fever.[1] It was a simple matter to pass between the fictional worlds of cinema and war, and Cecil B. De Mille, for example, lost no time in improvising as an army captain. The studio contingent formed the 'Lasky Home Guard'. Every Thursday evening, sporting rifles from the prop room and uniforms from the costume department, the big studio family paraded behind a band along Hollywood Boulevard. Mrs De Mille and Mary Pickford, for their part, dressed up as pretty nurses and wandered the streets in amazement that they could find no one wounded. Douglas Fairbanks and Charlie Chaplin harangued huge crowds in Wall Street, even though their simple megaphones did not carry far enough for them to be heard. But the crowd did not mind, being used to silent film and secretive statesmen. Won over by the actors' dumb show, people parted with their War Loan dollars more readily than they would have done for any politician.[2]

It is said that by the time De Mille was finishing *The Ten Commandments*, he imagined he was God himself leading the Jewish people. His dictatorial attitude to his family and friends and to the crowd of extras whose lives he often liked to put in danger did indeed suggest a man possessed, and his assumption of divinity involved a kind of charismatic infallibility stemming from foreknowledge of scripts which, as it happened, sometimes did not even exist. For a whole generation of cinematic miracle-workers, the process of direction, even if improvised, literally took the form of *revelation* – that is, divine action which makes known to men truths that they would not be able to discover by themselves.

At the same time, in Western Europe and the Soviet Union, a new breed of military and revolutionary leader was beginning to have a similar charismatic effect on the masses. These men were heralds of the *trans-political era*: since real power was now shared between the logistics of weaponry and of sound and images, between war cabinets and propaganda departments, as Abel Ferry already feared in 1914, parliamentary power had disappeared. 'Propaganda is my best weapon', declared Mussolini. And this is how Rosavita described the Duce: 'Go, Caesar . . .! Your task is fulfilled. From Caesar has come Benito Mussolini, strong and powerful as History has never before displayed; *his will partakes of the supernatural, the Divine, the miraculous, of Christ among men.*'[3] Just as unexpectedly, when Hitler was asked in private who was his great historical model, his answer was not Bismarck, as one might have thought, but Moses.

Perhaps it has not been properly understood that these miracle-working dictators no longer ruled but were themselves *directors*. In his final speech at the Nuremberg trial, Albert Speer stated:

> Hitler's dictatorship was the first in an industrialized state, a dictatorship which, in order to dominate its own people, used all technical means to perfection . . . thus, the criminal events of recent years were not due only to Hitler's personality. The enormity of these crimes may also be explained by the fact that Hitler was the first who used the means offered by technology to commit them.

The cinema was one of these means.

> When Hitler was crossing Munich by car in the autumn of 1939, he discovered that his favourite cinema, the *Fern Andra*, had changed its name. This sent him into a wild fury.[4]

Hitler, who closely observed the crowds flocking to celebrate the black masses of cinema, declared one day in 1938: 'The masses need illusion – but not only in theatres or cinemas. They've had all they can take of the serious things in life.' The Nazi *Lebensraum* was less the fulfilment of Bismarck's grand political schemes – although these formed the substance of Hitler's speeches – than the transformation of Europe into a cinema screen, for a people 'suddenly horrified by the everyday, the ordinary, and fascinated by the unusual' (Leni Riefenstahl).

Hitler violated only everyday realism, and the very nature of his crimes cannot be understood unless we remember his extraordinary technical knowledge of stage-direction, trick photography, trapdoor devices, revolving stages and, above all, the varied potential of illumination and floodlighting. 'Hitler may not have been the great statesman we saw in him,' argues Albert Speer, 'but he was and remains a psychologist whose like I have never encountered. Even as supreme army commander, he thought more about the psychological effect of a weapon than about its operational force'. (This from Speer, whose achievements included the Stuka sirens and the A4 missile warheads.)

In the same vein, according to the writer Jay Doblin, Hitler was 'the trademark designer of the century'. The swastika, for example, releasing potent affective associations, could not be confused with any other symbol – its stark simplicity still has an arresting power, as so much graffiti continues to prove. Hitler himself is said to have had a certain power of hypnotic suggestion: 'You knew something was false, but it became true because he said so', recalls the director Veit Harlan, who goes on to note the Führer's penchant for fakirism, his relations with Hanussen, and a certain conversation with Emil Jannings concerning his own personal safety: 'You see, Herr Jannings, when I'm speaking in front of a crowd, it's as if I'm taking in air. During this time, my defensive powers are fully active . . . no one will ever take a shot at me; that will work for as long as I like, for as long as I operate my dissuasive powers.' Harlan tells us that he subsequently began to observe Hitler with the closest attention, thinking of the possibilities that breathing offered to an actor. He noticed that the Führer's hypnotic power only operated in real life; it was not present in his pictures, nor did it work in his countless newsreel appearances.

In order to carry out his political project, Hitler required the services of film-makers and entertainers. But his greatest need was for those who could make the German people a mass of *common visionaries* 'obeying a law they did not even know but which they could recite in their dreams' (Goebbels, 1931). Thus, while Roosevelt's New Deal America was using radio and film to regulate the 'war of the home market' and to restart the industrial production machine, Hitler was directing the millions of unemployed Germans to relaunch war as an epic. Others would make war to win, but the German nation and its masters already moved in a world 'where nothing has any meaning, neither good nor evil, *neither time nor space*, and where what other men call success can no longer serve as a criterion' (Goebbels).

In 1934 Hitler called on Leni Riefenstahl to make *Triumph of the Will*, offering the young director an unlimited budget, a hundred and thirty technicians and ninety cameramen (to be placed on specially built lifts, turrets and platforms). All this to film the week-long congress of the National-Socialist Party in Nuremberg, and to spread the Nazi myth around the world with a film of unprecedented magnificence. Amos Vogel points out in this connection:

> . . . the most startling aspect of the project was the *creation of an artificial universe that looked entirely real* and the resulting production of the first and

most important example ever of an 'authentic documentary' of a pseudo-event. It is a stupendous revelation to realize that this whole enormous convention was primarily staged for the film.[6]

In *Hinter den Kulissen des Reichs-Parteitag-Films*, Leni Riefenstahl writes:

Preparations for the congress were fixed in conjunction with preliminary work on the film – that is to say, the event was organized in the manner of a theatrical performance, not only as a popular rally, but also to provide the *material* for a propaganda film . . . *everything was decided by reference to the camera.*

At the same time, Hitler put the architect Albert Speer in charge of constructing the 'real' sets for his political superproduction. Speer was appointed Inspector-General of Architecture, and after Fritz Todt's death in 1942 he became planner-in-chief of the total war.

These two assignments were less contradictory than they might appear, as Speer explained in 1938 in his *Theory of the Value of Ruins*. For Speer, the architect had a cinematic function similar to that of the military commander – namely, the capacity to determine in a building *what is permanent and what is impermanent.* In the last analysis, he argued, to construct a building is to foresee the way in which it will be destroyed, and thus to secure ruins which, thousands of years later, 'will inspire as many heroic thoughts as the models of Antiquity do today.' In the same year Hitler and Speer, no doubt impatient to imagine the future decor of the tragedy on which they were working, ordered the demolition of the centre of Berlin. Before becoming a battlefield, it was to be a premature field of ruins.

Speer's own architectural work, which is inspired by Boullée's Cyclopaean projects and the Baths of Caracalla, hardly outlived the film-sets of *Intolerance* – to take one example – which were once judged 'too expensive to pull down'. In fact, it was not long before Speer gave up construction and contented himself with *projecting* his architecture. Thus, when Hitler asked him to design a giant-scale vista for the Zeppelinfeld rally-stadium in Nuremberg, he laid aside his sketches of stone pillars and installed a hundred and fifty searchlight columns reaching up to the sky. Visitors to the stadium had the sense of being in a hypostyle theatre with a ceiling six thousand metres high, all of which would vanish into thin air at the first glimmer of daybreak.

When the *Blitzkrieg* finally flashed over Europe, German studios went on producing those sentimental films which audiences had already enjoyed long before the Nazis came to power – even though Goebbels wanted a realist cinema with strong popular features. The stepped-up production of

musical comedies, fairy tales and *Heimatfilme* (films exalting country life
and the 'simple, vigorous' German man) indicated that there was a rear-
base cinema, but the living cinema of the City's immortals was the 'steel
front' of Guderian's or Rommel's tanks and combat troops, the martial
isobar repeating the founding rites of *Festung Europa*.

A cameraman was attached to each platoon of the German army, and
these gifted, intrepid men succeeded where Griffith had failed in the First
World War. Each regiment had its own PK (Propaganda Company)
responsible for gathering and immediately processing information – a
kind of coordinating committee for film–army–propaganda, or pictures–
tactics–scripts.

'Many people ask themselves in wonder how an event taking place
hundreds of kilometres away in the heart of enemy territory can, the very
next day, be the subject of radio news reports', wrote a *Berliner Illustrierte
Zeitung* journalist in 1941. Quite genuine newsreel footage was used as
the basis for whole films such as *Feuertaufe* (*Baptism of Fire*), an account
of the Nazi invasion of Poland designed to sow terror among foreign
audiences and to make them recognize the superiority of the German
army. 'The images have no immediate dramatic tension, but the simplified
montage of more or less disparate associations and the running
commentary should beam out to the audience their vibrating rhythm of
great historical events.'[7] PK cinema was thus built on the work of Leni
Riefenstahl, for whom everything in her films was true although it took
place in *intensive time* similar to the real time of Blitzkrieg, to the actual
speed of military technology.

In 1943 the ageing Franklin Roosevelt, his powers diminished by the
illness that would soon carry him away, carelessly declared total war at
the end of the Casablanca Conference.[8] The Allied air forces were now
free to practise a new strategy of zone bombing, whose aim was to oblit-
erate not just military targets but entire regions. Operation Gomorrah
went on to consume the city of Hamburg in a fire-storm and to unleash
apocalyptic floods in the Ruhr, while the mass of German survivors–
extras were flung into a pan-cinema as total as the war itself. Strangely
enough, the population responded to this war as to an ever grander spectacle, one capable of matching the cataclysmic biblical scenes of Hollywood epics. Spurning any petty thoughts, they resolved to work sixteen
hours a day if the Führer should so command.

What is officially known as the 'total war speech' was delivered on the
historic date of 18 February 1943. It was then that the close associates
Speer and Goebbels, architect of ruins and minister of propaganda,
decided to override the Party dignitaries who, like Hitler himself, were
against an escalation of the situation. Speaking to a rally at the Berlin
Sports Palace, Goebbels in effect addressed the whole of German society:

'The English claim that the German people does not want total war but capitulation. I ask you, do you want total war? Do you want it to be still more total, more radical than we can imagine it today?' The tragic affirmative of the enraptured crowd left the way clear for the *Gauleiter* to conclude: 'Well then, people of Germany, let the storm break!' War now spread not just territorially but to the whole of reality, with neither limits nor purpose.

In the course of the terrible winter of 1942–43, Paulus's Sixth Army was encircled and destroyed in the decisive battle of Stalingrad that marked the beginning of the great Soviet counter-offensive. At the end of 1943 Berlin lay crushed beneath Allied bombs. Many German leaders were by then convinced that defeat was inevitable.

As immediate successes became rarer and rarer, Hitler decided to provide his public with a flash-back to earlier victories. The director Veit Harlan[9] was ordered to make a film in Norway about the bitter fighting that had taken place three years before in Narvik between British and German forces, General Dietl being asked to replay his own role in the capture and occupation of the town. When Harlan arrived at Narvik Fjord, the rusted hulls of German torpedo-boats and British ships could still be seen jutting out of the water, and the town itself was no more than a mass of ruins in which soldiers of the Reich survived as best they could. The British immediately learned of Hitler's grand film-project and were aware that he had promised Harlan several warships and a hundred aircraft to parachute in thousands of men. Cinema was thus about to turn Narvik – which had been a stinging and face-losing blow for the British – into a most interesting target of operations. For why should they too not take part in a remake, with a different ending?

London therefore announced over the radio that if Veit Harlan wished to film the battle, the Home Fleet would set up some particularly realistic and bloody scenes for the camera. The German soldiers, notwithstanding their devotion to the Führer, showed little enthusiasm: 'To die for the fatherland struck them as more logical than to die for the cinema!' noted Harlan. 'It appears that Admirals Raeder and Dönitz made representations to Hitler, as well as to Goering. They won their case and the project so emphatically ordered by Hitler was put in cold storage.' Goebbels, deeply disappointed, confided to the director that the whole business could have yielded a feast of exciting documentary film – and that he had planned to send a team of newsreel reporters if the British did intervene.

Shortly afterwards, on 28 October 1943, shooting began on *Kolberg*. At a time when the German army was retreating on all fronts, the Führer once again demanded that it should be placed entirely at the disposal of the film-makers; that was a *military order*. In a context of universal shortages, six thousand horses and nearly two thousand men were committed to the battle scenes, and waggon-loads of salt were brought up to simulate the snow that had to cover the harbour jetty. Districts of Kolberg were reconstructed in the vicinity of Berlin so that they could be bombarded by 'Napoleon's cannons', while the capital itself lay devastated by Allied raids. Six cameras, including one on a boat and another in the basket of an anchored balloon, simultaneously filmed the capture of Kolberg, as thirty detonation experts set off a huge number of explosions. It was even decided to create a flood by diverting the river along specially built canals and triggering underwater charges by electrical remote-control. By January 1945, however, when the film was ready to be shown, Berlin's first-run cinemas were no more than a heap of rubble.

On the 30th of April, Hitler finally departed his 'hell of images', by committing suicide in the camera obscura of the Reichskanzlerei bunker.

Eye-witnesses have recalled that in those final days he laid the plans for a 'new Berlin' to rise from the ruins like the Lumière Brothers' wall. As for the 'common visionaries' of the Third Reich, a strong course of denazification was introduced to wake them up. Survivors began to say that they could not understand what had happened to them; the Faurissons of this world would soon be swearing that it had never taken place.

Our concern here, of course, is not with film history but with the osmosis between industrialized warfare and cinema. At this level, the most serious war films are sometimes the most comical, but in the early part of the century military technology itself still had an element of buffoonery. In 1929 there was more than a touch of Méliès in Fritz von Opel's powder-fuelled rocket-plane that took off from Frankfurt aerodrome, or in the jet-propelled sledges designed by Max Valier.

Nor is there much difference between the science fiction of the young Werner von Braun, and Théa von Harbou's and Fritz Lang's script for *A Woman on the Moon*. As to the impoverished schoolteacher Hermann Oberth, whose work on rocketry met with mocking incomprehension, he could almost have been the fictional hero of the latter undertaking. For it was only the hope of UFA financial backing for his *real experiments* that drove Oberth to collaborate on the technical planning of the film, and in the end Lang himself paid half the cost of Oberth's experiments in order to put an end to the producers' doubts and haggling.

The film came out on 30 September 1929, but without the intended publicity of a real rocket launch from the beach of Horst in Pomerania to an altitude of forty kilometres. By 1932 jet technology, being developed at Dornberger's newly opened Kummersdorf West Research Centre, was set to become one of the major military secrets of the Third Reich, and the German authorities of the time seized Lang's film on the grounds that it was *too close to reality*. A decade later, on 7 July 1943, von Braun and Dornberger presented Hitler with film of the real launch of the A4 rocket.

The Führer was in a bitter mood: 'Why was it I could not believe in the success of your work? If we'd had these rockets in 1939 we'd never have had this war.'[10]

Only recently has it been realized that the Allies' victory in the Second World War was at least partly due to their grasp of the real nature of Nazi *Lebensraum*, and to their decision to attack the core of Hitler's power by undermining his charismatic infallibility. They did this by making themselves the leading innovators in film technology.

Technological mystery now replaced the mystery of the film-script and tended to become the defining concept of real war. Thus, in the extraordinary story of Enigma, and its technological counter Ultra, the Anglo–German battle over decoding machines changed the direction of the war.[11] The decisiveness of battle had been overtaken by the sheer scale of what could be brought into play. When Napoleon (or Griffith) created a battlefield, he was able to concentrate prevision and decision in one act of looking, and without neglecting detail he could re-establish organization and control with unequalled speed. But when Napoleonic warfare spread to the vast expanses of Russia in 1812, drawing in half a million men on the French side alone, this type of visual organization underwent logistical collapse. Long gone were the days when Frederick II and a few others managed to see 'life-sized' shapes forming and developing on the field, in as regular a battle order and in as geometric patterns as had been earlier drawn up on paper. Armies were now composed of numerous mobile units which struggled hard to establish contact in the course of the action, responding to orders given outside their own field of vision.

To grasp the objective truth of a great battle, the camera-eye (of Napoleon or Griffith) could not have been that of the general or the director. Rather, a monitor would have had to have recorded and analysed a number of facts and events incomparably greater than what the human eye and brain can perceive at a given place and time, and then to have inscribed the processed data onto the battlefield itself. The level of foresight required by the geopolitical dimensions of modern battlefields demanded a veritable meteorology of war. Already we can see here the video-idea that the military voyeur is handicapped by the slowness with which he scans a field of action overstretched by the dynamic revolution of weaponry and mass transport. Only the further development of technology could offset this tendency to which it had given rise. For the disappearance of the proximity effect in the prosthesis of accelerated travel made it necessary to create a *wholly simulated appearance* that would restore three-dimensionality to the message in full. Now a holographic prosthesis of the military commander's inertia was to be communicated to the viewer, extending his look in time and space by means of constant

flashes, here and there, today and yesterday ... Already evident in the
flash-back and then in feed-back, this miniaturization of chronological
meaning was the direct result of a military technology in which *events
always unfolded in theoretical time*. As in cinema, what happens is
governed not by a single space–time principle but by its relative and
contingent distortion, the capacity for repressive response depending upon
the power of anticipation.

Abel Gance understood this perfectly in 1914.

6

*Sicut Prior est Tempore ita quo Potior Iure**

Rest never comes for those transfigured in war. Their ghosts continue to haunt the screens or, most frequently, find reincarnation in an engine of war – usually a ship, like the *Tirpitz*, which sank in a fjord in 1943 and whose technological metempsychosis was celebrated in a feature film. Admiral William Nimitz, the American commander-in-chief of naval aviation in the Pacific from 1942 to 1945, gave his name to a nuclear aircraft-carrier which featured in another recent film, Don Taylor's *The Final Countdown* (1980). In this work of science fiction, whose theme is war across time, the Japanese fleet is steaming towards Pearl Harbor when it is detected by the *Nimitz*, which has been carried back half a century by a disturbance in the space–time vortex. The ship's commander faces a dilemma: whether to let history take its course, or to block the attack on Pearl Harbor by using all the fire-power at his command.

The most interesting thing in this film is the new crisis of decision-making that results from the non-peaceful coexistence of different technologies. Where are the orders to come from? From the commander of Pacific forces who, in 1941, knows of no vessel by the name of *Nimitz*? Or from the commander of US Defense, in 1980? As with the planned film *Narvik*, we can see here a determination to extend military power on both sides of a hypothetical 'time centre' by using relativity as a military manoeuvre. In the film, the nuclear carrier *Nimitz* acts as a watchtower across historical time: the means of communication and identification employed in modern warfare become ways of blocking history. The new media allow the viewer to sense the *differential time-span* borne by each technological object. The effect is a startling temporal relief, such that the

---

*'Priority in time gives priority in law.' Roman adage.

engine of war restores the material war-time of military–industrial propaganda in which we are the involuntary protagonists.

The British, who had invented the 'Fleet in Being' to rule the waves as well as vast continents, allocated enormous sums during the inter-war period for research into communications and detection, and were particularly receptive to this kind of retro-prospective effect. In 1930, the British actor Leslie Howard had made a strangely premonitory film, *Outward Bound*, in which a number of passengers find themselves on board an aeroplane without knowing the destination. Eventually it becomes clear to them that they are already dead and that the craft is simply transporting them into the next world. Thirteen years later, on 1 June 1943, a DC-3 Ibis on which Leslie Howard happened to be travelling also vanished without trace.

Back in October 1939 Howard had a hard time persuading Whitehall to help him make propaganda films in Britain. 'Why don't you do that in the United States?' he was asked. 'We're short of everything here.' Instead, he was offered a liaison job similar to Noel Coward's work for the French government on the interpretation of Nazi propaganda.[1] Howard turned this down and submitted a proposal of his own:

> The first film that I want to make is a documentary of the British White Paper on the outbreak of war. I want to put it out as a film record, using some newsreel stuff, but acting the real parts. There is a theme I want to bring home. Let me explain – I am working on a simple principle: that the mind will always triumph over brute force in the long run.

When he was asked which role he would play, he replied:

> Oh, acting Hitler for a start, and then I want to play Sir Nevile Henderson myself. The last bid for peace against the tactics of Ribbentrop. . . . You see, nobody abroad wants to read official documents now. They won't buy your White Paper. But they will crowd into the cinemas to see an official documentary.[2]

Howard's attempts at persuasion ended in failure, but they led to the conception of Pimpernel Smith – the absent-minded professor who bamboozles the Nazis – which demonstrated Howard's ideas in a rather flippant style that he did not particularly like. Howard went on to make a number of propaganda films, including *The First of the Few* which featured some of the best pilots from the Battle of Britain (Townsend, Bader, Cunningham) in an account of the life of Spitfire designer R.J. Mitchell.

In 1943 Lubitsch presented *To Be or Not To Be* to American audiences – a film which, though largely inspired by Howard's misfortunes, aroused considerable indignation in the United States. For this was the year of Roosevelt's declaration of total war, and people preferred to see Hitler vanquished by Superman than by some unknown and rather shabby-looking Shakespearian actors. The film had an equally bad reception when it was shown in France in 1954, and yet this 'disrespectful fantasy' was really a serious war film – disturbing, too, in its exposure of the philosophy of the Allied Special Services. British defence secrets, protected by a censor's office that was to remain in place for more than thirty years, really did reside as much in Shakespearian theatre as in the headquarters of the armed forces. For example, the plan for Montgomery's famous victory over Rommel at El-Alamein was drawn from *Macbeth* by a film director, Geoffrey Barkas, and a music-hall magician, Maskeline, the two men reproducing Malcolm's action at Birnham Wood. Over the hard sand of the desert, virtually devoid of landmarks, the British army moved so slowly that the enemy's sharpest look-outs, equipped with the best field-glasses, could detect no real advance.

The British were soon to have another stroke of genius. Since the chronophotographic reconnaissance of the First World War, information had greatly depended upon central analysis and interpretation, and Whitehall well knew that German Intelligence, reconstituted in the thirties by Theo Rowehl, a close friend and ex-naval colleague of Admiral Canaris, had an insatiable appetite in such matters. The Luftwaffe's bombers and reconnaissance aircraft were at once engines of destruction and engines of cinema, movie producers, as it were, filming not only the battlefield but also the territory of the United Kingdom itself. Rather than attempt to interfere with this, the Allies therefore decided to take part in the *mise en scène* of Hitler's newsreel and intelligence films. Their main technique was not classical camouflage but, on the contrary, overexposure. Enemy cameras were offered sight of scenery, matériel, troop movements – all part of the almost limitless repertoire of visual illusions in real space.

At the crucial point when massive preparations were under way for the Normandy landings, the East Anglian countryside came to resemble an enormous film lot complete with Hollywood-style props. Men with imagination, such as the architecture professor Basil Spence, were assisted in their work of visual disinformation by a mass of painters, poets, theatre and cinema technicians. Famous studios like Shepperton near London went over to producing phoney armoured vehicles or landing ships.

Smoke coiled from [the landing ships'] funnels, they were surrounded by oil patches, laundry hung from the rigging, motorboats left wakes from ship to ship, and intruding aircraft could see their crews – over-age or unfit soldiers of units such as the 10th Worcestershires and the 4th Northamptonshires. Thousands of carefully shielded truck lights indicated the presence of large convoys, and lights over 'hards' gave the impression of intense loading activity after dark. And behind this 'invasion fleet', which was large enough to 'land' the entire 1st Canadian Army, which did not as yet exist, the fields of East Anglia and Kent were crowded with tanks, guns, half-tracks, ammunition dumps, field kitchens, hospitals, troop encampments and fuel lines. They, too, were fakes.[3]

The sound-track was also well worked out, with all the care of a film script. It contained various brief, misleading, dialogues that could be picked up by German radio-operators across the Channel – apparently part of the normal run of military signals. And to add a final touch of authenticity, public figures, including King George himself, and Generals Eisenhower and Montgomery, were invited to visit the spurious docks, ships and building-sites. At other key moments, look-alikes of Churchill and other military leaders embarked on aeroplanes to undertake bogus trips.

This relationship between actors and statesmen, like the grotesque substitution scenes of *To Be or Not To Be*, clearly reveals the kind of war stratagems thought up by the Allies to mystify Hitler and the German high command about the real course of operations against the Third Reich, to leave the enemy bewildered as well as beaten.

After 1945, Britain's wartime services kept up their role of monitoring the varied scripts of international propaganda, with their attention now turned to the countries of the Eastern bloc. Technicians easily switched from special army measures to special cinema effects, and the old studios at Shepperton continued to house scale models and science-fiction devices.

> During the summer and fall of 1978, a visitor to England's Shepperton Studios might have found that making the forty-five minute drive back to London would be easier than trying to get past the main gate. Four of Shepperton's massive sound-stages – one of them is amongst the largest in the world – were housing the sets for *Alien*. Twentieth Century Fox wanted to make sure that the sixteen weeks of principal shooting would only be witnessed by authorized eyes . . . The movie's biggest secret would be kept.

Roger Christian, the film's art director, adds: 'Ridley showed us *Dr Strangelove* and he kept saying, "That's what I want. Do you see? Not that it's a B-52 in outer space, but it's the military look." I knew what he was saying because I had done it in *Star Wars*.'[4] Like many cinema ships and vehicles before it, *Nostromo* in *Alien* contained a host of real features from World War Two battleships, tanks and bombers: 'For instance, we made a control panel out of airplane junk and about a million switches.'

On screen, science-fiction vessels become bright and sonorous plastic, a kind of thorough technological mix which, as with real military equipment, was designed to give the effect of synthesis to a variety of more or less anachronistic components. 'Film criticism no longer has any meaning,' Hans Zischler, one of Wim Wenders's actors, recently said to me; 'it is *reality* that we have to analyse in a cinematic way.' Evidently verisimilitude is no longer assured with the new engines of war: military technology has advanced too far out of our sight, its secrecy revives for us the attraction of faraway lands, and the wish for proximity is repeating the old imposture of immediacy. With its dreamlike design, its much-caressed contours, the machine's body pursues the derangement of its appearances. The most intense hope seems to have moulded its particular form – a hope in which aerodynamics suddenly loses its value as a science of air flow and becomes a logistical pantheism of time flow.

Back in the forties Orson Welles once said: 'For me, everything that's been called direction is one big bluff. Editing is the only time when you can be in complete control of a film.'[5]

Francis Coppola, a great admirer of Abel Gance, shared his passion for the techniques of military commanders and their way of eliminating random factors. After the seventies' vogue for electronic effects, which allowed a considerable reduction in the 'natural', objective uncertainties of scenery and machinery, Coppola and quite a few others began to use the electronic prerecording of both sound and image to suppress any element of chance. Thus, shooting no longer involved the rigorous placement in time and space of the old *Kammerspiel*. As in radio productions, the actors played out their roles in the studio, and the director then worked ad lib on his editing table shuffling and inserting the various shots. 'In this way,' Coppola remarks, 'he gets the most sophisticated possible result for the least price.'[6]

Coppola has developed in an interesting direction since the partial disappointment of *Apocalypse Now*. In fact, the emotional *One from the Heart* is more of a war movie than *Apocalypse Now*, and it is quite clear that this new film art in which actors and sets vanish at will is an art of extermination. Coppola directly uses military equipment like the Xerox 'Star' naval computer system, and his cost-benefit approach is like the attitude of a modern army to miniaturization or automation, which is seen as 'transferring the possibility of human error from the point of action to the design and development process'.[7]

Thus, the last power left to the director, as to the army officer, is not so much to imagine as to foresee, simulate and memorize simulations. Having lost material space, the bunkered commander of total war suffers a loss of real time, a sudden cutting-off of any involvement in the ordinary world. Like the new opaque cockpits which prevent fighter pilots from

looking outside, because 'seeing is dangerous', war and its technologies
have gradually eliminated theatrical and pictorial effects in processing the
battle image, and total war followed by deterrence have tended to cancel
the scenario effect itself in a permanent technological ambience devoid of
any substratum. With the new composites, the world disappears in war,
and war as a phenomenon disappears from the eyes of the world. Crew
members on the aircraft carrier *Nimitz* recently told a journalist from
Libération: 'Our work is totally unreal. Every now and then, fiction and
reality should get together and prove once and for all that we are really
here.'

Total war takes us from military secrecy (the second-hand, recorded truth
of the battlefield) to the overexposure of live broadcast. For with the
advent of strategic bombing everything is now brought home to the cities,
and it is no longer just the few but a whole mass of spectator-survivors
who are the surviving spectators of combat. Nuclear deterrence means
that there are no longer strictly 'foreign wars'; as the mayor of Philadelphia put it twenty years ago, frontiers now pass through the middle of
cities. Berlin, Harlem, Belfast, Beirut, Warsaw and Lyon . . . the streets
themselves have now become a permanent film-set for army cameras or
the tourist-reporters of global civil war. The West, after adjusting from the
political illusions of the theatre-city (Athens, Rome, Venice) to those of
the cinema-city (Hollywood, Cinecittà, Nuremberg), has now plunged
into the transpolitical pan-cinema of the nuclear age, into an entirely cinematic vision of the world. Those American TV channels which broadcast
news footage around the clock – without script or comment – have understood this point very well. Because in fact this isn't really news footage any
longer, but *the raw material of vision*, the most trustworthy kind possible.
The extraordinary commercialization of audiovisual technology is
responding to the same demand. For videos and walkmans are reality and
appearance in kit form: we use them not to watch films or listen to music,
but to add vision and soundtracks, to make us directors of our own
reality.

Even back in the fifties and sixties, when people were asked why they
flocked to pop concerts or festivals like Woodstock, they used to say it was
because they didn't want to hear themselves think, or because at such
events there was no longer any real distinction between spectators and
performers. Hundreds of thousands of actor–spectators went to stadium
cycloramas, where the cameras and lasers illuminated not just the stars
but also the wildly excited crowds. Those who came to watch also
exhibited themselves, in a way heralding such spectacular actions of the
seventies as the assassination of John Lennon.

Today, directors (and politicians) have lost all prominence, and are swallowed up in technical effects, rather like Nicholas Ray in Wim Wenders's *Lightning Over Water.* 'We get our energy from chaos', the Rolling Stones once said. And from everyday terrorism to live-broadcast assassinations, the living pan-cinema is spreading before us that chaos which was once so well concealed by the *orderly* creation of war. Even if our actions are suddenly slipping out of their usual frames of reference, they are not *actes gratuits* but cinema-acts.

With the neutron bomb, urban populations have lost their ultimate value as nuclear hostages and have been abandoned by military planners. There are no more 'immortals of the City'. And cinema itself has lost its initiatory value and ceased to be the black mass of martial aboriginality which can offer cinematic Valhalla to the children of the fatherland in a communion of the quick and the dead. For the commercial distribution of video and audio equipment is destroying the extraordinary technical capacity of the old cinema to shape society through vision, to turn a thousand film-goers into a single spectator.

7

A Travelling Shot over Eighty Years

This story could have begun in 1854, at the siege of Sebastopol during the Crimean War, or seven years later with the American Civil War, since in both conflicts abundant use was made of modern techniques: repeating weapons, photographic records, armoured trains, aerial observation . . . But I have chosen to start in 1904, the first year of the 'war of light'. For it was then, a year after the Wright brothers flew in the *Kitty Hawk*, that a searchlight was used for the first time in history, in the Russo–Japanese war.

Trained on the heights of Port Arthur, the focused incandescence of war's first *projector* seemed to concentrate all the torches and all the fires of all the wars before it. Its beam pierced more than the darkness of the Russo–Japanese war; it illuminated a future where observation and destruction would develop at the same pace. Later the two would merge completely in the target-acquisition techniques of the *Blitzkrieg*, the cine-machineguns of fighter aircraft, and above all the blinding Hiroshima flash which literally photographed the shadow cast by beings and things, so that every surface immediately became war's *recording* surface, its *film*. And from this would come directed-light weapons, the coherent light-beam of the laser.

A number of events combined to make 1904 a historic year. First of all, it witnessed the death of Etienne-Jules Marey, that key link in joining together repeater-guns and repeater photography, whose chronophoto-graphic rifle was, as we have seen, both precursor of the Lumière brothers' camera and direct descendant of the Colt revolvers and cylindrical guns. The multi-barrelled Gatling gun, invented at the start of the American Civil War, ended its military career in 1904 at the siege of Port Arthur, although an electronic version re-entered active service in Vietnam.

In 1904, too, Marey's assistant, Georges Demeny, then a member of a commission working on an infantry manual, published L'Education du marcheur in which he showed the usefulness of chronophotography in proportioning the soldier's expenditure of effort (forced marches, handling of weapons, etc.). Demeny later played an important role in the physical training of the French army before 1914.

Finally, on 18 May 1904 in Cologne, Christian Hülsmeyer tested his 'telemobiloscope', which could alert a remote observer to the presence of metallic objects – the forerunner, in effect, of radio-telemetry and Watson-Watt's 'radio detection and ranging' (Radar).

If we remember that it was an optics professor, Henri Chrétien, whose work during the First World War perfecting naval artillery telemetry laid the foundations for what would become Cinemascope thirty-six years later, we can better grasp the deadly harmony that always establishes itself between the functions of eye and weapon. And, indeed, while the advance of panoramic telemetry resulted in wide-screen cinema, so the progress of radio-telemetry led to an improved picture: the radar picture, whose electronic image prefigured the electronic vision of video. From the commanding heights of the earliest natural fortifications, through the architectonic innovation of the watch-tower, and the development of anchored observation balloons, or the aerial reconnaissance of World War I and its 'photographic reconstruction' of the battlefield, right up to President Reagan's latest early warning satellites, there has been no end to the enlargement of the military field of perception. Eyesight and direct vision have gradually given way to optical or opto-electronic processes, to the most sophisticated forms of 'telescopic sight'. The strategic importance of optics was already clear in World War I, one indication being the dramatic rise during the war in French production of optical glass (for rangefinders, periscopes and camera lenses; for telemetry and goniometry) – from 40 tonnes to 140 tonnes a year, half the total Allied output.

The idea of war as fundamentally a game of hide-and-seek with the enemy was proved to the point of absurdity in those First World War earthworks where millions of men were entrenched and interred for four long years. With the appearance of what came to be called saturation weapons (repeating rifles, machine-guns, rapid-firing field guns) firepower alone determined who would be victorious – rather than the disposition of troops, the strict geometry of their movements. All efforts were made to conceal and disperse one's forces instead of deploying them in maximum concentrations. Hence those endless waves of sacrificial infantrymen who leapt over the parapets and crawled through the mud to their own burial – dead or alive, but anyway safe from enemy eyes and guns.

If the First World War can be seen as the first mediated conflict in history, it is because rapid-firing guns largely replaced the plethora of

individual weapons.¹ Hand-to-hand fighting and physical confrontation
were superseded by long-range butchery, in which the enemy was more or
less invisible save for the flash and glow of his own guns. This explains the
urgent need that developed for ever more accurate sighting, ever greater
magnification, for *filming the war* and photographically reconstructing the
battlefield; above all it explains the newly dominant role of aerial observation in operational planning.

In the wars of old, strategy mainly consisted in choosing and marking
out a theatre of operations, a battlefield, with the best visual conditions
and the greatest scope for movement. In the Great War, however, the
main task was to grasp the opposite tendency: to narrow down targets
and to create a picture of battle for troops blinded by the massive reach of
artillery units, themselves firing blind, and by the ceaseless upheaval of
their environment. Hence that multiplicity of trench periscopes, telescopic
sights, sound detectors, and so on. The soldiers of the First World War
may have been actors in a bloody conflict. But they were also the first
spectators of a pyrotechnic fairy-play whose magical, spectacular nature
some of them could already recognize (I am thinking especially of Ernst
Jünger, Apollinaire and Marinetti). Ten years after the siege of Port
Arthur, this was the inauguration of total war, a continuous performance,
all day and all night.

Indeed, why should there have been any rest after dark? For the
enemy's presence made itself known only through the flash of gunfire or
the glow from the trenches, and daytime blindness was hardly any different from that which set in at nightfall. As a prelude to the lightning war
of 1940, here was a *lighting war*, with the use of the first tracer bullets,
flares that lit up no-man's-land for nocturnal targets, powerful searchlights with a range of nine kilometres, and early anti-aircraft defence
systems. The old adage, 'The cavalry lights the way, the infantry wins the
day', now well and truly belonged to the past. As the front settled into
positional warfare, aviation took over the cavalry's functions and reconnaissance planes became the eyes of the high command, a vital prosthesis
for the headquarters strategist, illuminating a terrain that was constantly
being turned upside down by high explosives. Landmarks vanished: maps
lost all accuracy. And as the landscape of war became cinematic, so the
first on-board cameras came into their own. For only the lens-shutter
could capture the film of events, the fleeting shape of the front line, the
sequences of its gradual disintegration. Only serial photography was
capable of registering changing troop positions or the impact of long-
range artillery, and hence the capacity of new weapons for serial destruction.

Marey's interest in disclosing the successive phases of a body movement here becomes a concern to explain the sequence of a sudden disinte-

23. Cameraman in the fore-turret of a Lancaster bomber, 1943.

24. Photo taken during the night bombing of Essen on 4 April 1943. The special effects, called silver shrouds by Allied air crews, were part of the intensive German air-defence system.

25. British Pathfinder Force pilots inspecting the results of their night raids on Germany in 1943.

26. Mission board of the US air reconnaissance.

27. Switching cameras in the nose of a US twin-engine F-5: Mount Farm, England, 1 July 1943.

28. Pilot climbing aboard his twin-engine aircraft.

29. *I.* Pre-flight synchronization test of camera and aircraft speeds at Mount Farm, ensuring that the rhythm of machine-gun fire will automatically determine the spacing of photographs and thus leave the pilot free to navigate. *II.* Result of the film test.

30. A Spitfire's flight and photographing schedule.

FEATURE LINE OVERLAPS – STRAIGHT 30 EXPOSURES.

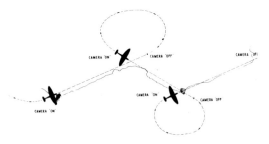

FEATURE LINE OVERLAPS – ADVANCED

QUICK TURN ON SIDE BETWEEN EXPOSURES & CORRECT DIRECTION

IMPRACTICABLE WITH SHORT TIME INTERVAL

31. Flight plan, giving direction and altitude, to ensure good photographic cover of the military target.

32. American officers examining aerial reconnaissance prints as they come out of a Williamson multiprinter at Mount Farm. 1 July 1943.

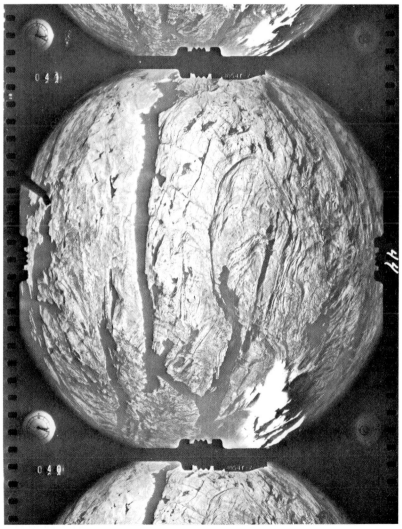

33. Aerial film of Norway, taken in 1943 with 142° lens.

34. A 'Trimetrogon' system (one upright and two sloping cameras) on board a USAF B-17.

35. Cameraman cleaning the glass lens-cover of a 'Trimet' sloping camera on board a B-17.

36. The Hughes XF11, prototype of a reconnaissance aircraft developed by Howard Hughes in 1944. Two years later, Hughes crashed it on a test flight in Beverly Hills.

37. Field photo-laboratory of the US Army. Chattanooga, 1940.

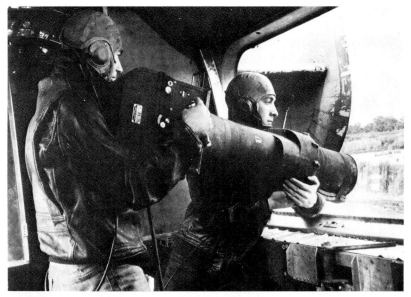

38. Fitting a camera on a Liberator. Guadalcanal, 1943.

39. Small US Navy laboratory at Rendova in the Solomon Isles, June 1943. The camouflage indicates that it is close to the front.

40. Laboratory at Guadalcanal, 1943. An officer is handing over wide-reel film to be destroyed.

41. American photo-analysis of the raid on Weimar-Buchenwald on 24 August 1943. The dark-shaded buildings were thought to have been seriously damaged. The concentration camp, in the upper right of the picture, was not hit.

TRINITY SITE
WHERE
THE WORLD'S FIRST
NUCLEAR DEVICE
WAS EXPLODED ON
JULY 16. 1945
ERECTED 1965
WHITE SANDS MISSILE RANGE
J. FREDERICK THORLIN
MAJOR GENERAL U.S ARMY
COMMANDING

42. Monument in the Oscura Peak area of White Sands Desert.

43. The city of Jericho, as depicted in the Hebrew Bible. (Farhi Bible, 1366/1382. Rabbi Solomon, Sassoon Library, Jerusalem.)

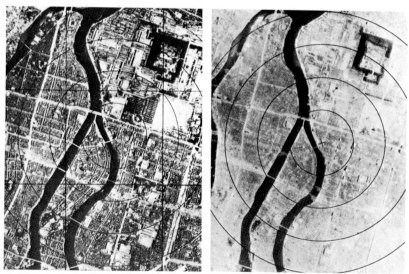

44. Photographs of Hiroshima before and after the first nuclear bombing in history, 6 August 1945.

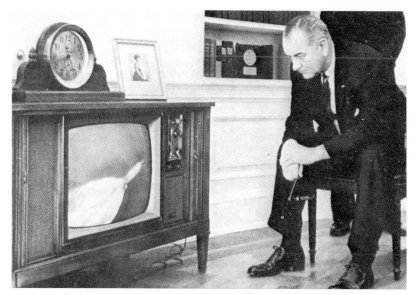

45. President Lyndon Johnson in the White House watching the Saturn I rocket take off on 29 January 1964. As André Malraux wrote: 'Caesar could have conversed with Napoleon, but Napoleon has nothing to say to President Johnson.'

46. The War Room in Stanley Kubrick's *Dr Strangelove*.

Prise par Lunar Orbiter-5 le 8 août 1967,
cette image a été téléphotographiquement transmise
par framelets : pour la première fois,
un cliché de la Terre était obtenu
depuis la région lunaire.
Une grande partie du Vieux Continent
est visible : le terminateur
coïncide approximativement
avec le 135ᵉ méridien est.

47. Photograph of the Earth relayed from Lunar Orbiter, 8 August 1967.

gration of the landscape which is not fully visible to any one person. Aerial photography, cinematic photogrammetry – once again we find a conjunction between the power of the modern *war* machine, the aeroplane, and the new technical performance of the *observation* machine. Even though the military film is made to be projected on screen, thus obscuring the practical value of the successive negatives in analysing the phases of the movement in question, it is fundamentally a reversal of Marey's or Muybridge's work. For the point is no longer to study the deformations involved in the movement of a *whole body*, whether horse or man, but *to reconstitute the fracture lines of the trenches, to fix the infinite fragmentation of a mined landscape alive with endless potentialities*. Hence the crucial role of photographic reconstruction, and of those military films which were the first, little-known form of macro-cinematography, applied not (as with Painlevé after 1925) to the infinitely small but to the infinitely large. Thus, as the Hachette *Almanach* of 1916 put it, the techniques of representation proved their enormous importance during the war: 'Thanks to negatives and films, it was possible to retrace the whole front with the greatest clarity, from Belfort to the Yser.'

On the one hand, the secret of victory is written in the air by the ballistics of projectiles and the hyper-ballistics of aeronautics; on the other, it is negated by speed since only the speed of film exposure is capable of recording that military secret which each protagonist tries to keep by camouflaging ever larger objects (artillery batteries, railways, marshalling yards, and eventually whole towns as the black-out belatedly responded to the lighting war of 1940).

Just as weapons and armour developed in unison throughout history, so visibility and invisibility now began to evolve together, eventually producing *invisible weapons that make things visible* – radar, sonar, and the high-definition camera of spy satellites. The Duke of Wellington once said he had spent his life guessing what was on the other side of the hill. Today's military decision-makers don't have to guess: their task is to avoid confusing the forms of a representation which, while covering the broadest regions of the front, must take in the minute details always liable to influence the outcome of a conflict. The problem, then, is no longer so much one of masks and screens, of camouflage designed to hinder long-range targeting; rather, it is a problem of ubiquitousness, of handling simultaneous data in a global but unstable environment where the image (photographic or cinematic) is the most concentrated, but also the most stable, form of information.

The camera-recording of the First World War already prefigured the statistical memory of computers, both in the management of aerial observation data and in the ever more rigorous management of the simultaneity of action and reaction.

Was the Bofors predictor of the Second World War not the forerunner of the 'strategic calculator' of the immediate post-war period? In this anti-aircraft gun, which improved on telemetry by making the ballistic trajectory coincide with the target aircraft at a certain point in time and space, the deadly result was achieved by means of stereoscopic superimposition, in real time, of the two flight images on a screen.

Thus, the theatre of operations of the Napoleonic Wars, where actors in the bloodbath moved in rhythm and hand-to-hand fighting was conducted by the naked eye and with bare weapons, gave way at the beginning of this century to a camera obscura in which face-to-face confrontation was supplanted by instant interface, and geographical distance by the notion of real time.

Military strategy had earlier involved the division of space, the building of permanent fortifications complete with ditches, ramparts and screens that added up to what one nineteenth-century general called 'a kind of box of surprises'. The twentieth century moved on to the division of time, where the surprise effect came from the sudden appearance of pictures and signs on a monitor, and where screens were designed to simulate, rather than dissimulate, a war that ever more closely resembled non-stop cinema or round-the-clock television. Only with the Second World War and the spread of radio-telephony, however, did the silent cinema of radio-telegraphy finally begin to talk.

In *Steel Storms*, published in 1920, Ernst Jünger draws on his experience at the Front to express this derealization effect of industrialized warfare:

> In this war where fire already attacked space more than men, I felt completely alien to my own person, as if I had been looking at myself through binoculars . . . I could hear the tiny projectiles whistling past my ear as if they were brushing an inanimate object. . . . The landscape had the transparency of glass.

This total transparency affecting object, subject and surrounding space – which makes each of the antagonists feel both that he is watched by invisible stalkers and that he is observing his own body from a distance – illustrates the derangement of perception in an environment where military technology is distorting not only the battlefield, but also, and especially, the space–time of vision, where the observation machine and the modern war machine are conjoined to such a degree that Jünger can say: 'The faculty of thinking logically and the sense of gravity seemed to be paralysed.'

The radar operator later had this same sensation of looking down from a great height, and it was to cancel this human element that scientists developed 'True Motion Radar' which eliminated any optical image from the monitor. What the video artist Nam June Paik calls the triumph of the electronic image over universal gravity has carried this still further. The sense of weightlessness and suspension of ordinary sensations indicates the growing confusion between 'ocular reality' and its instantaneous, mediated representation. The intensity of automatic weaponry and the new capacities of photographic equipment combine to project *a final image of the world*, a world in the throes of dematerialization and eventual total disintegration, one in which the cinema of the Lumière brothers becomes more reliable than Jünger's melancholy look-out who can no longer believe his eyes.

A highly meaningful incident from the First World War – one which, curiously enough, repeated itself twenty-six years later in a variant itself indicative of the changing battlefield – will confirm the truth of this argument. In 1914 the French and German commands had little faith in aerial observation and greatly preferred the use of ground patrols. At the Battle of the Marne, however, Captain Bellenger, the man in charge of aviation in the fortified area around the capital, responded to General Gallieni's urging and stepped up the number of reconnaissance flights in the vicinity of Paris. A conflict of interpretation then broke out between Gallieni, a specialist in colonial wars who excelled in the use of new technology, and the officers responsible for the front. Seen from the ground, the direction of the German offensive was unclear and the reports of scouts were contradictory (although the general staff took them as gospel). Seen from the sky, the axis or general thrust suddenly became apparent, but the French high command refused to accept the evidence and quite naturally set greater store by horizontal, perspectival vision than by the vertical, panoramic vision of overflying aircraft. Eventually Gallieni imposed his 'point of view' on enemy movements – not in Paris, but on the Marne. Some writers ascribed the resulting victory at the first battle of the Marne to the Paris region's dense, concentric railway network with its efficient *regulation of traffic*. Today, however, it seems at least plausible that the happy outcome also depended upon *regulation of points of view* – that is, on a definition of the battle image in which the cavalry's perspective suddenly lost out to the perpendicular vision of the reconnaissance aircraft.

Henceforth, as Winston Churchill confirmed, the general tendency prevails over successive episodes. It is like the difference between the invention of cinematography and the invention of chronophotography: since armed clashes could now only be perceived through *projection*, only the photogramme of the war film could reveal their inner dynamic or general line, ground patrols being left to serve as a tactical control. The system of reviewing images and sequences in accelerated motion was then applied to military reviews and exercises, on a training ground which was no more than a screen for projection of the war of movement. Alone capable of making visible the likelihood of attack, cinema became associated with battle in the same way that telescopic sights were attached to rifles or the cine-machine-gun to aerial warfare.

The *Blitzkrieg* brought home this reversal of perspective in a repetition of the episode from the Marne. In the course of spring 1940 – on the 10th of May, to be precise – events followed one another with such rapidity that only the air force could grasp their catastrophic dimensions. On the 12th of May, in a report now kept in the French Air Force archives, Lieutenant Chery from Reconnaissance Group 2/33 (the one in which Saint-Exupéry served) wrote as follows: 'The bridges over the Meuse are intact. Overall impression: the enemy is advancing with armoured divisions in the Ardennes, and is meeting no resistance.' Despite this clear-cut information, the French general staff refused to believe the lieutenant-observer. An old military axiom – 'Ardennes: non-strategic, impenetrable country' – had stopped the Maginot Line from being continued northward, and thus there could be no question of lending credence to Chery's heretical communication. The sequel is well enough known. The issue here is no longer the scale of the point of view but how pervious certain terrain is to the advance of enemy ardour.

The glass-like transparency of Jünger's war landscape is thus compounded by the piercing of dense country, such that a wooded massif becomes transparent to rolling armoured divisions. This is no longer merely an *optical illusion* affecting a soldier suffering psychic weightlessness; rather, it is a *motor illusion* affecting strategic territory that offers no more resistance to tanks than air space does to dive-bombers.

In his writings as a war pilot, Saint-Exupéry uses some arresting metaphors:

> All I can see on the vertical is curios from another age, beneath clear, untrembling glass. I lean over crystal frames in a museum; I tower above a great sparkling pane, the great pane of my cockpit. Below are men – protozoa on a microscope slide. . . . I am an icy scientist, and for me their war is a laboratory experiment.[2]

The soldier's panic-stricken distancing from static warfare is transferred to the technology of lightning-war, to the telescopic lenses and the stereoscopic glass of military photo-analysis, in a medium which seems aqueous, glass-like, with all its phenomena of refraction and diffraction.

Positional warfare, then, had had its day. The extreme mobility of mechanized armies imparted a new temporal unity that only cinema could apprehend, albeit with occasional difficulty since the greater speed of aircraft extended the flow of images and high altitudes iced up the camera's mechanism. For these reasons, military scientists refined optical scanning methods, assisted the pilot's fallible memory with a tape-recorder while awaiting the onboard computer, and made filming more precise by means of a 'hyposcope' that could readily visualize the aircraft's vertical. Heavy and cumbersome sheet-emulsion was replaced by self-winding film cartridges. Air speed/film speed adjustors, in-flight marking of negatives and the coupling of photo-electric cells made it easier to interpret documentary output and thus further improved its quality.

The limits of investigation, in both time and space, were being pushed back. The rapid movement of armies meant that their advance had to be detected at the furthest possible point within an aircraft's range, so that the command would have sufficient time to respond. Gone were the times of the four-kilometre-an-hour infantry, when information remained fresh for a day, a week or even more. Now reports lost their value within a few hours, or even a few minutes. If the secrets of war are always written in the air, only high-speed transmission allows their importance to be usefully deciphered.

After the defeat of France, the British took Sidney Cotton's advice and reorganized their aerial reconnaissance by replacing the heavy, weapons-carrying Blenheim bombers with unarmed Spitfires that could load a spare fuel-tank. This state-of-the-art aeroplane, performing like a veritable flying camera, prefigured today's 'video-missiles' which are capable of detecting, live or in play-back, not only the succession but also the simultaneity of various actions.

It was in 1912 that the German Alfred Maul launched a powder-fuelled rocket with a small photographic device in its nose cone. When it reached its highest point, the rocket took a single photograph and came back to earth at a slower speed (a military experiment which built upon Nadar's first aerostatic pictures). Twenty years later at RCA's laboratories, Vladimir Zworykin invented the 'Iconoscope', the first name for the electronic television. He presented it not as a mass medium but as a way of expanding the range of human vision – indeed, anticipating the Pioneer and Voyager space probes by many years, he even wanted to place a camera on a rocket to observe inaccessible regions.

This urge to expand the range of vision and detection eventually found a scientific answer in the electro-magnetic radar beam, which at the time of the Battle of Britain gave the air the transparency of ether. Watson-Watt spread out a mysterious, invisible screen in the atmosphere, reaching to such a height that no air vessel could pass through without being detected somewhere on the ground, in the form of a blob of light in a darkened room. What had once taken place in the darkroom of Niepce and Daguerre was now happening in the skies of England. The war room in London filled up with senior officers and female assistants – hostesses, one might say, of a strategic office imitating real war – who organized the flow of 'Chain Home' radar information and coordinated the RAF combat formations. Brief exchanges between crews and their 'war hostesses' passed through the ether, as if the couples were together in the same room. Duly warned, guided and consoled, the fighter-pilots were ceaselessly followed by these offstage voices. It was not only the war film that had become a talkie. For the pilots could visualize the audience in the operations room and punctuated their brilliant feats of arms with exclamations and commentaries. The female assistants contributed to their leader's success, as well as to the derealization of a battle in which ghosts played an ever greater role – screen ghosts of enemy pilots served to confirm that they had been shot down, and ghostly radar images, voices and echoes came through on the screens, radios and sonars. The projection of light and waves had replaced the old projection of arrows and javelins.

Although military force depends on its relationship to outward appearance, this power has over the years lost its verisimilitude in a profusion of camouflage, decoys, jamming, smoke-screens, electronic countermeasures, and so on. The offensive arsenal has equipped itself with new devices for a conflict in which optical and motor illusion have fused in the cinematic delirium of lightning-war. Here what counts is the speed at which objects, images and sounds travel through space, until the moment of the nuclear flash.

In the spring of 1940, unlike 1914–18, reconnaissance aircraft had a constant short-wave radio link with the ground, over a range that would increase from a few dozen kilometres to five hundred by the end of the war. In the autumn of the same year, RAF night-fighters became the first to have onboard radar which enabled pilots to see on cockpit screens a Dornier or Messerschmitt-110 flying through the dark over five kilometres away. The pilot's gift of double sight thus introduced a new doubling of the warrior's personality: with his head up, atmospheric transparency and ocular targeting; head down, the transparency of the ether, long-distance vision. Two military spaces, one close and one faraway, corresponded to a single battle, a single war. Later these technologies led to the development of over-the-horizon weapons systems.

As for the night-bombers, which had to face the blinding light of 200 million candlepower searchlights, they gradually acquired new resources and procedures to help them accomplish their mission. Whereas in 1940 the Luftwaffe dropped incendiaries to mark the bombing area in London and Coventry, in 1941 the Allies' 'Operation Millennium' used impact flare-bombs to sketch out in the darkness a rectangle of red lights for the Halifaxes and Lancasters to release their destructive load over Cologne.

Subsequently the Allies developed the magnesium flare and the electronic flash, which allowed USAF bombers not only to light up the ground but, more importantly, to dazzle enemy defences for a few moments. (Such innovations were taken further by Sam Cohen in the Vietnam War, when it became possible to blind the enemy for more than an hour: the latest development in this line is the stun grenade used against terrorists in Mogadishu and London.)

By 1942 ground-based electronic devices were able to direct Flying Fortress squadrons over a very long distance, helping them to drop their bomb-loads by day or night and under any weather conditions. The two ground stations involved were known as 'The Cat' and 'Mickey Mouse'. Aircraft fitted with a special receiver picked up the cat's beam and let themselves be passively guided to the vicinity of the target. The mouse, which had so far followed the operation in silence from a distance of some four hundred kilometres, then took over and, having calculated the moment when the bomber should release its load, transmitted the instruction by radar – all with a margin of error of a mere hundred metres.

This sophisticated electronic network covering Western Europe was first known as GEE. But as it continually improved, its name changed to the call-sign OBOE and finally, in 1943, to H2S, by which time it could give pilots not just a radar signal but a 'radar image', a luminous silhouette of the target over which they were flying. The bombing apparatus was equipped with a transmitter that beamed centimetric waves in a perpendicular line to ground level, the echoes then returning and forming on a cathode screen an electronic image of fifteen square kilometres. The system was used for the first time in Operation Gomorrah, which devastated Hamburg.

The visible weapons systems of artillery, machine-guns, and so forth thus became entangled with the invisible weapons systems of a continent-wide electronic war. No longer were objects on the ground invisible to pilots, who in the past had related to natural conditions both as a source of protective concealment from enemy fire and as a hindrance that masked their own target. Anti-aircraft defences benefited in turn from the ubiquitousness of war: the Kammhuber Line, for example, whose operational centre was at Arnhem in Holland, organized the German fighter response with an air-raid warning system that covered key areas from the North Sea to the Mediterranean. A network of 'panoramic radar' installations, each tracking a circle of three hundred kilometres, could cable an electronic image of the sky to the anti-aircraft batteries of *Festung Europa*. This total visibility, cutting through darkness, distance and natural obstacles, made the space of war translucent and its military commanders clairvoyant, since response time was continually being cut by the technological processes of foresight and anticipation.

The air-raid alert system also played a major psychological role on the Continent. Advance warning could be given to civilian populations as soon as enemy squadrons crossed the coast, and this was translated into a full-scale alert once they veered towards their target city. With the compression of space–time, danger was lived simultaneously by millions of attentive listeners. For want of space to move back into, their only protection was time given to them by the radio.

The Allied air assault on the great European conurbations suddenly became a *son-et-lumière*, a series of special effects, an atmospheric projection designed to confuse a frightened, blacked-out population. In dark rooms that fully accorded with the scale of the drama, victims-to-be witnessed the most terrifying night-time fairy theatre, hellish displays of an invading cinema that reproduced the Nuremberg architecture of light. Albert Speer, organizer of the Nazi festivities at Zeppelinfeld, wrote as follows of the bombing of Berlin on 22 November 1943:

> The raid offered a spectacle whose memory cannot be erased. You constantly had to remember the appalling face of reality if you were not to let yourself be entranced by this vision. Parachute-rockets – 'Christmas trees', as Berliners called them – suddenly lit up the sky; then came the explosion whose glare was engulfed by the smoke of incendiaries. On every side, countless searchlights scoured the night and a gripping duel began when an aeroplane, caught in the pencil of light, tried to make its escape. Sometimes it was hit and for a few moments became a blazing torch. It was an imposing vision of apocalypse.

Hitler's architect was well placed to measure the small distance from the hell of images to the image of hell:

> For the Nuremberg Party Congress in 1935, I used 150 anti-aircraft searchlights whose perpendicular, skyward beams formed a luminous rectangle in the night. Within these walls of light, the first of their kind, the congress unfolded in all its ritual. It was a fairy-like decor, reminding one of the glass castles imagined by poets in the Middle Ages. I now have a strange feeling when I think that my most successful architectural creation was a phantasmagoria, an unreal mirage.

Not a mirage, but rather a dress rehearsal for the war, a holographic harbinger which used material available to the army for more than thirty years.

Transparency, ubiquitousness, instant information – it was the time of the great 'command operas' where, in London as in Berlin, stage-directors moved the naval and air fleets around. 'The headquarters transmission centre was a model of its kind,' writes Speer.

From his table in the conference room, Hitler was able to command all the divisions on the fields of battle. The worse the situation became, the more this instrument of modern warfare served to underline the divorce between reality on the ground and the fantasy which presided over the conduct of operations at that table.[3]

Commanders were now able to exercise their authority with a minimum of go-betweens. Hitler acted the warlord by radio-telephoning orders to his generals and depriving them of initiative, but in the end the whole system of communications, in both camps, worked to strengthen the supreme commander's control over his subordinates. *Power was now in a direct link-up.* If, as the strategist Se-Ma put it, an army is always strong when it can come and go, move out and back, as it pleases, we have to say that in this period of war the comings and goings were less those of troops than of the output from detection and transmission equipment. Visual or audiovisual technology now began to reproduce not only the forced march or distant incursion – as it did in the 1914–18 war – but the actual movement of armies, with automatic feed-back and retransmission in real time. How else can we understand the introduction of PK units in the Wehrmacht, or the Allied armies' use not just of war correspondents but of their own cine-commando units – how else but by the need for ever more advanced mediation of military action, so that the pilot's 'gift of double sight' could be extended to a high command at once absent and omnipresent?

In making attack unreal, industrial warfare ceased to be that huge funeral apparatus denounced by moralists and eventually became the greatest mystification of all: an apparatus of deception, the lure of deterrence strategy. Already in the Great War, as we have seen, the industrialization of the repeating image illustrated this cinematic dimension of regional-scale destruction, in which landscapes were continually upturned and had to be reconstituted with the help of successive frames and shots, in a cinematographic pursuit of reality, the decomposition and recomposition of an uncertain territory in which film replaced military maps.

Cinematic derealization now affected the very nature of power, which established itself in a technological Beyond with the space–time not of ordinary mortals but of a single war machine. In this realm sequential perception, like optical phenomena resulting from retinal persistence, is both origin and end of the apprehension of reality, since the seeing of movement is but a statistical process connected with the nature of the segmentation of images and the speed of observation characteristic of humans. The macro-cinematography of aerial reconnaissance, the cable television of panoramic radar, the use of slow or accelerated motion in analysing the phases of an operation – all this converts the commander's plan into an animated cartoon or flow-chart. In the Bayeux Tapestry, itself

a model of a pre-cinematic march-past, the logistics of the Norman landing already prefigured *The Longest Day* of 6 June 1944.

Now, it should not be forgotten that inductive statistics developed from
the calculations that Marshal Vauban used to make during his long and
repetitive journeys to the same place at different times. On each of these
trips, Louis XIV's commissioner-general of fortifications became a kind of
'commissioner for displays'.[5] The kingdom paraded before his eyes, offering itself up for general inspection. This was not just a troop muster for the
logistical benefit of the officer in charge of army comportment; it was a
full-scale review of the country, a medical examination of its territorial
corpus. Instead of the ordinary situation in which serried ranks used to
pass back and forth before the watchful gaze of the king's administrator, it
was the country's provinces, drawn up as on parade, which were passed in
review by his inspector-general. However, these repeated trips, which
caused the regional film to unwind, were no more than an artifice or cinematic trick for the sole benefit of the itinerant observer. Alone as he
watched the situations and sequences dissolve, he gradually lost sight of
local realities and ended up demanding a reform of fiscal law in favour of
administrative norms.

Statistics brings us to the dawn of political economy, which rested on
the persistence of the sign and of dominant trends, not on the merely
chronological succession of facts. It is the same movement of ideas which
led from the Enlightenment to photographic recording, Muybridge's
multiple chambers, Marey's chronophotography and the Lumière
brothers' film-camera, not forgetting Méliès, the inventor of the mystification of montage.

Winston Churchill, it is well known, believed that whereas episodic
events used to have greater importance than tendencies, in modern wars
the tendency had gained the upper hand over episodes. Mass phenomena
do indeed elude immediate apprehension and can only be perceived by
means of the computer and interception and recording equipment which
did not exist in earlier times (hence the relative character of Churchill's
judgement). We should therefore conclude that total war has made an
essential contribution to the rise of projection equipment which can reveal
and finally make possible the totalitarian tendencies of the moment.

The development of 'secret' weapons, such as the 'flying bomb' and
stratospheric rockets, laid the basis for Cruise and intercontinental
missiles, as well as for those invisible weapons which, by using various
rays, made visible not only what lay over the horizon, or was hidden by
night, but what did not or did not yet exist. Here we can see the strategic
fiction of the need for armaments relying on atomic radiation – a fiction
which, at the end of the war, led to the 'ultimate weapon'.

As we saw in the first chapter, many epilogues have been written about the nuclear explosions of 6 and 9 August 1945, but few have pointed out that the bombs dropped on Hiroshima and Nagasaki were *light-weapons* that prefigured the enhanced-radiation neutron bomb, the directed-beam laser weapons, and the charged-particle guns currently under development. Moreover, a number of Hiroshima survivors have reported that, shortly after it was detonated, they thought it was a *magnesium bomb* of unimagined power.

The first bomb, set to go off at a height of some five hundred metres, produced a nuclear flash which lasted one fifteen-millionth of a second, and whose brightness penetrated every building down to the cellars. It left its imprint on stone walls, changing their apparent colour through the fusion of certain minerals, although protected surfaces remained curiously unaltered. The same was the case with clothing and bodies, where kimono patters were tattooed on the victims' flesh. If photography, according to its inventor Nicéphore Niepce, was simply a method of engraving with light, where bodies inscribed their traces by virtue of their own luminosity, nuclear weapons inherited both the darkroom of Niepce and Daguerre and the military searchlight. What appears in the heart of darkrooms is no longer a luminous outline but a shadow, one which sometimes, as in Hiroshima, is carried to the depths of cellars and vaults. The Japanese shadows are inscribed not, as in former times, on the screens of a shadow puppet theatre but on a new screen, the walls of the city.

A-bomb, 1945; H-bomb, 1951. Korean War. . . . After the war everything speeded up: firepower referred not just to firearms but to the jet-pipes of fighter aircraft. The sound barrier was crossed in 1952, the 'heat barrier' in 1956. As to the light barrier, that was for later. In the skies, Strategic Air Command bombers were in constant readiness, and Air Defense Command interceptors spread their protective umbrella for the eventuality of a Soviet long-range attack. The danger was all the greater in that the USSR exploded its first hydrogen bomb on 12 May 1953.

For the United States, it was becoming an urgent matter to have new information-gathering methods at its disposal. And so it was that Eastman Kodak came up with its Mylar-based film and Dr Edwin Land of Hycon Corporation with the high-resolution camera – both of which laid the basis for regular aerial reconnaissance over the Soviet Union. The sequel is well known. October 1961 saw the beginning of the Cuban crisis, with the threat of a third world war. On 29 August 1962, a U-2 aeroplane came back from a mission over Fidel Castro's island with film evidence of Soviet missile installations. This sparked off the confrontation between Khrushchev and Kennedy which, after several months, led to a hot-line link-up between the two heads of state, an instant interface between their operations rooms.

We should remember that the U-2, still in service over Iran and the Persian Gulf, is fitted not only with photographic and electronic surveillance systems but also with a telescopic collimator or 'cine-drift indicator' which allows the spy pilot to follow ground contours at a height of more than twenty-five thousand metres.

Also in 1962, at a time when there were already ten thousand American advisers in Vietnam, the first electronic war in history was devised at Harvard and MIT. It began with the parachute-drops of sensors all along the Ho Chi-Minh Trail, and continued in 1966 with the development of the electronic 'MacNamara Line', consisting of fields of acoustic (Acouboy, Spikeboy) and seismic (Adsid, Acousid) detectors spread along the Laos access routes, around US army bases and especially the Khe Sanh stronghold.

At that time Harvard Professor Roger Fisher developed the strategic concept of a 'land-air dam', relying on up-to-the-minute technology to keep an effective watch on enemy movements. It would use infra-red devices and low-lighting television, combined with the most advanced means of aerial destruction such as the F-105 Thunderchief fighter, the Phantom jet, and the Huey-Cobra helicopter gunship. Transport aircraft (the Douglas AC-47 and, above all, the Hercules C-130) were converted into flying batteries with the latest electronic equipment: laser targeters capable of guiding bombs with absolute precision; a night-vision and image-enhancer system; and computer-controlled, multi-barrelled Minigums, descendants of the old Gatling gun which could fire six thousand rounds a minute.

With this sophisticated alert-system, made necessary by the fact that enemy movement usually took place by night, the black-out was a thing of the past, and darkness the fighter's best ally, while the daylight theatre also became a darkened cinema for the shadowy combatants. Hence the Americans' frenzied efforts to overcome this blindness by having recourse to pyrotechnic, electrical and electronic devices, most of which employed light intensification, photogrammetry, thermography, infra-red scanning, and even specially invented infra-red film. All these weapons systems resulted in a new staging of war, massive use of synthetic images, and automatic feed-back of data. They also gave rise to chemical defoliation, whereby it finally became possible to empty the screen of parasitic vegetation.

In October 1967, the Nakhon Phanom electronic surveillance centre in Thailand was picking up, interpreting and displaying on screen data sent from ground-interceptors and relayed by Lockheed Bat-Cat aeroplanes. In these offices, the new nodal point of the war, an IBM 360.35 computer automatically sorted the data, producing a 'snapshot' which showed the time and place when the interceptors had been activated. On the basis of this information, analysts drew up a schedule of enemy movement and passed on to fighter-bomber crews the 'Skyspot' combat data that enabled them to go into action with the greatest dispatch and precision. Most interesting from our point of view, however, was the pilotless Drone, an aircraft with a wing-span of approximately three metres whose camera could take two thousand pictures and whose onboard television could broadcast live to a receptor station 240 kilometres away.

'*Il pleut mon âme, il pleut mais il pleut des yeux morts*',[6] wrote Apollinaire in 1915, referring to enemy fire. With the advent of electronic warfare, this figure has become out of date. Projectiles have awakened and opened their many eyes: heat-seeking missiles, infra-red or laser guidance systems, warheads fitted with video-cameras that can relay what they see to pilots and to ground-controllers sitting at their consoles. The fusion is complete, the confusion perfect: nothing now distinguishes the functions of the weapon and the eye; the projectile's image and the image's projectile form a single composite. In its tasks of detection and acquisition, pursuit and destruction, the projectile is an image or 'signature' on a screen, and the television picture is an ultrasonic projectile propagated at the speed of light. The old ballistic projection has been succeeded by the projection of light, of the electronic eye of the guided or 'video' missile. It is the life-size projection of a film which would have overjoyed Eugène Promio, the inventor of the travelling platform, and even more Abel Gance, who wanted to launch his cameras like snowballs into the Battle of Brienne.

Ever since sights were superimposed on gun-barrels, people have never stopped associating the uses of projectiles and light, that light which is the soul of gun-barrels. Recent inventions have included the photon accelerator and the light intensifier, and now there are the laser weapons, directed beams, charged-particle guns, and so on. Not content with barrel-mounting, the experts have inserted a sighting device into the inner tube of artillery in order to improve performance. At ballistic and aerodynamic research laboratories in both France and the United States, 'hyperballistic firing tunnels' nearly a hundred metres long can launch scale-models of 're-entry bodies' (the projectiles being tested) at a speed of 5,000 metres a second. 'Cineradiographic' flash equipment, with a capacity for 40 million images a second, is then used to visualize their path in the bore of the gun.[7] This takes us back to the origins of cinema, to Marey's first chrono-photographic rifle which had a lens in the barrel and a cylinder for moving round the light-sensitive plate.

Since Vietnam and throughout the seventies, the mediation of battle has grown ever more pronounced. At the time of the Korean War a USAF Sabre already required more than forty kilometres to turn a Mig-15, but in Vietnam (as in the Six Days War) a Phantom needed an instrument-backed firing system if it was to have any hope of bringing down a Mig-21. The Phantom's targeting system subsequently led to the 'Fire and Forget' concept and to the Over-the-Horizon weapons systems which allow an attack to be conducted off the field.

The disintegration of the warrior's personality is at a very advanced stage. Looking up, he sees the digital display (opto-electronic or holographic) of the windscreen collimator; looking down, the radar screen, the onboard computer, the radio and the video screen, which enables him to follow the terrain with its four or five simultaneous targets, and to monitor his self-navigating Sidewinder missiles fitted with a camera or infra-red guidance system. However, this war of the waves had some major drawbacks, as Colonel Broughton, an F-105 Thunderchief pilot in Vietnam, has explained:

> The radio chatter was really picking up about this time – in fact, it was so dense with all the Mig and Sam warnings and everyone shouting directions and commands that it was almost impossible to interpret what was going on. This is a real problem and once it starts, it just keeps getting worse and worse and is almost impossible to stop . . . you see something that you know you have to tell other people about in a desperate hurry to protect them and to protect yourself, and the temptation is to blurt it out as quickly as possible without using the proper call sign. The result is that everyone in the air immediately gets a shot of confusion and wonders who is talking about whom.[8]

Such confusion was often exacerbated by poor weather conditions in North Vietnam:

> The weather over there is the thickest I have ever seen and when you get inside one of those big thunder-bumpers you are in for a good ride. Most clouds you fly through have their share of bumps but the visibility inside is usually good enough so that you can sit on the wing of another aircraft and fly formation off him. You just maintain the position you want and when he turns or rolls his aircraft, you roll right along with him. You have no idea where you are if you are on the wing, but that is up to the leader. The only time you get into trouble on the wing is when you try to fly position and also try to outguess the leader. This usually winds up in a case of spatial disorientation called vertigo. If this happens you can be sitting straight and level and swear that you are cocked up in a 60-degree bank going sideways. It is a most distressing sensation and sometimes almost impossible to get rid of. You can shake your head and holler at yourself and sometimes it won't go away, and it can be fatal. . . . For a real thrill, I recommend you try this type of flying on a black night.[9]

The weightlessness that Ernst Jünger felt during artillery barrages in the First World War is reproduced in this account. However, the confusion of sensations involves not a panic-stricken terror but a technological vertigo or purely cinematic derealization, which affects the sense of spatial dimension. Tied to his machine, imprisoned in the closed circuits of electronics, the war pilot is no more than a motor-handicapped person temporarily suffering from a kind of possession analogous to the hallucinatory states of primitive warfare. We should not forget that the first stimulants were developed in response to the needs of Luftwaffe pilots.

Narcotics were to become the plague of the US expeditionary corps in Vietnam. From the beginning, they suffered from the hallucination of technological combat-delirium, which blurred the distinction between the real and the imaginary. In this war of images, Broughton writes:

> Unfortunately, the groups known as photo interpreters are not always of the highest level of skill or experience, and their evaluation quite often does not agree with that of the men doing the work. I have bombed, and seen my troops bomb, on specific targets where I have watched the bombs pour in and seen the target blow up, with walls or structures flying across the area, only to be fragged right back into the same place because the film didn't look like that to the lieutenant who read it way back up the line. I have gone back on these targets and lost good people and machines while doing so, and found them just as I expected, smashed. But who listens to a stupid fighter pilot?[10]

People used to die for a coat of arms, an image on a pennant or flag; now they died to improve the sharpness of a film. War has finally become the third dimension of cinema.

It is a curious fact that much of the new matériel – helicopter gunships, missiles, telecommunications, detection systems – was being produced by the Hughes Aircraft Company, whose celebrated founder, Howard Hughes, had directed a film in 1930 about a First World War bomber crew (*Hell's Angels*). This schizophrenic magnate, who died in 1976, built an industrial empire by associating cinema and aviation, and Hughes Aircraft remains today one of the largest companies in the United States. In 1983, for example, it was working on improvements to the TOW anti-tank missile's guidance system, introducing an optical tracking device that allowed missiles to be precisely aimed despite the pitching and vibrating of the helicopter from which they were fired. But it was also developing equipment for in-flight entertainment, making it possible for infra-red rays to carry music and films to the passengers of regular airlines and business jets.

After the Vietnam defeat, Pentagon scientists and industrialists did not give up their drive to perfect electronic warfare. The MacNamara Line was transferred to the south of the United States – or, more precisely, the border with Mexico – with the supposed aim of detecting illegal immigrant workers. As for the anti-personnel interceptors, they gave birth in 1971 to a wild plan sponsored by the National Security Agency for the development of a personalized tracking device that could be used by the police. This electronic 'transponder', as it was known, was designed to record the distance, speed and path of an offender's movements and to transmit the information several times a minute, via relay-receivers, to a central screen-computer. Having checked these data against the permitted itineraries, the computer could immediately alert the police if the person wearing the 'tracking bug' went elsewhere or tried to remove it. Although the original idea was to use it for prisoners on parole, this system of *electronic incarceration* finally enabled a kind of prison reform. The cell would be replaced by a tiny black box, by confinement to the shadows through the stage direction of everyday life.

In 1974, spurred on by the oil crisis, this process of derealization acquired fantastic proportions with the boom in military flight and combat simulators, which effectively took the place of the old 'home trainer'. The production of synthetic 'daylight' images had meant that at last pilots could be trained without interruption in all aspects of a combat mission, covering the customary phases of navigation, penetration and attack. An instructor could teach them not just to pilot an aircraft with instruments but to pilot a series of startlingly realistic images. This *mise-en-scène* of war led a few years later to an event that went unnoticed: namely, the recognition of an equivalence between simulator time and real flight time. If we bear in mind the strictness of certification procedures for aeroplane pilots, we shall better understand the importance of such a decision.

Today, techniques have improved still further and a 'dogfight simulator', consisting of two spherical cabins, can simulate an attack by two enemy aircraft. It should be noted at this point that simulation has long since spread to the other two branches of the military. The Sperry Corporation – one of the main manufacturers, together with Thomson, of this type of equipment – produces for armoured units as well as for the navy and the air force. Moreover, within the East–West framework of direct non-aggression that has resulted from the strategy of nuclear deterrence, military manoeuvres have also gradually taken on the aspect of large-scale electronic games, a *Kriegspiel* requiring whole territories over which the various procedures and materials of modern war are reconstituted.

In the Nevada Desert, a special practice range known as 'Red Flag' has been created to simulate exposure to a Soviet defence system. Authentic Soviet surface-to-air missiles and accompanying radar equipment – whether Israeli war booty or old supplies to Egypt – help to re-create a perfectly realistic electronic environment of radar beams, firing procedures, radio transmissions, and so forth, which the American crews are trained to recognize and then neutralize. The aerial force participating in such exercises includes an AWACS flying control-tower and an Aggressor

Squadron made up of aircraft whose features are similar to those of the Mig-21 and Mig-23. Similarly, in the Mojave Desert in California, the Army's National Training Center simulates war in the most life-like way. Thanks to 'Miles' (the Multiple Integrated Laser Engagement System), the soldiers' weapons on both sides project laser or infra-red rays with a range and trajectory roughly comparable to those of real ammunition. The various targets, fitted with silicon plates, are linked up to 'black boxes'. Both the troops and their weaponry also carry sensitive plates on their most vulnerable surfaces, so that when one is hit by a laser beam, the micro-processor in the black box calculates the impact and communicates it to Headquarters, which then adds up the score. A host of other simulation devices and special film effects complete the picture.

In the same order of ideas we should mention the Tactical Mapping System, a video-disc produced by the Advanced Research Project Army. By speeding up or slowing down the procession of fifty-four thousand images, and changing the direction or season as one might switch television channels, the viewer is able to build up a continuous picture of the small Colorado town of Aspen. The town is thus transferred to a sort of ballistic tunnel for tank-pilots, who use this method to train in street combat. Let us not forget that the Dykstraflex camera made by John Dykstra for the film *Star Wars* – a camera in the service of a computer which records its own movements – was actually descended from a pilot training system.

The same kind of technological spin-off lies behind the SPAACE camera, an automatic tracking system that two Frenchmen developed for the cinema on the basis of an anti-aircraft radar platform. This new-style camera, with its powerful telephoto lens, can follow the actors' spontaneous movements without any difficulty, even locking on to the face of a jet pilot executing a low-altitude figure. The fact is that once the energy crisis had made the simulation industry profitable, the pace of technological innovation grew more frantic towards the end of the seventies and culminated in the automation of the war machine.

The complexity of manoeuvres, the ever greater air speeds, the assistance of satellites, and the necessity for ground-attack aircraft to fly supersonically at very low altitudes eventually led the engineers to automate piloting itself. On the F-16 'AFT1', for example, developed by Robert Swortzel, the pilot never touches the controls but navigates by voice. In return, an on-screen display keeps him informed of his flight plan and 'firing plan' and throws up on the windscreen the anticipated acceleration and countdown time, as well as the kind of manoeuvres that the pilot will have to execute. For the firing operation, the pilot has a special sighting-helmet linked to a laser and infra-red targeting system; all he has to do is fix the target and give a verbal instruction for the weapons to be released.

This revolutionary apparatus, designed in 1982 for the United States Air Force, the Navy and NASA, combines a number of advanced technologies, particularly in the field of laser-targeting. The Eye-Tracked synchronization system fixes the pilot's gaze, however sudden the movement of his eyes, so that firing can proceed as soon as binocular accommodation is achieved.

Finally, there is the 'homing image', which joins together an infra-red ray and an explosive projectile fitted with a special device. This device acts in the manner of an eye, picking up the image of the infra-red-lit target. The projectile then makes its way towards the image – and thus towards the target for destruction – with all the ease of someone going home. This system, which is attached to the latest missiles, once again illustrates the fateful confusion of eye and weapon.

We can now understand better the concern on both sides to perfect weapons that are as undetectable as a submerged submarine – Stealth bombers, 'smart' missiles, invisible not just to the human eye but above all to the piercing, unerring gaze of technology. In the 1980s there was a significant shift or 'conversion' in global strategy, as East–West conflict passed into North–South confrontation. Notwithstanding the tensions in the Middle East and the Euromissiles controversy, military space is being shifted and organized around the oceans, in the Pacific, the Indian Ocean and the South Atlantic. Indeed, the Malvinas War can be seen as a rehearsal for a nuclear conflict, in the use of American and Soviet satellites, British nuclear submarines, and French missiles capable of destroying highly exposed surface-ships. But it was also a war of electronic countermeasures – naval decoys whose main feature was to superimpose upon the incoming missile's optical or infra-red radar image an entirely manufactured image that would appear both more important and more attractive than the real ship, as well as being equally credible to the enemy missile. Once this was achieved, the missile's automatic navigator locked on to the centre of gravity of the 'decoy-image-cum-ship-image', and all that remained was to exploit the spectre of the decoy to draw the missile far over the ship. The whole operation lasted barely a few seconds.

One could go on for ever listing the technological weapons, the panoply of light-war, the aesthetic of the electronic battlefield, the military use of space whose conquest was ultimately the conquest of the image – the electronic image of remote detection; the artificial image produced by satellites as they endlessly sweep over the surface of continents drawing automatic maps; life-size cinema in which the day and the light of film-speed succeed the day and the light of astronomical time. It is subliminal light of incomparable transparency, where technology finally exposes the whole world.

In the summer of 1982, the Israeli preventive war in Lebanon, baptized

'Peace in Galilee', drew on all the resources of the scientific arsenal: Grumman 'Hawkeye' aircraft-radar capable of simultaneously locating two hundred and fifty targets for F-15 and F-16 fighter-bombers; and, above all, the remote-piloted 'Scout' automata, with a wing-span of less than two metres, which were massively and systematically deployed for the first time in the history of battle. This toy craft, worthy of Ernst Jünger's *Glass Bees*, was a veritable Tsahal's eye fitted with TV cameras and thermal-image systems. As it skimmed the rooftops of the besieged city of Beirut, flying over the most exposed Palestinian districts, it provided images of population movement and thermal graphics of Palestinian vehicles for Israeli analysts sitting at their video consoles more than a hundred kilometres away.

In the autumn of 1982, the United States established a military high command for space and announced the impending launch of an early-warning satellite. In the spring of 1983, on 23 March to be precise, President Reagan painted a picture of an anti-ballistic-missile system employing nuclear energy, enhanced rays, directed beams and charged particles.

Last summer, on 5 July 1983, an American KC-135 aircraft fitted with a laser system shot down a Sidewinder missile travelling at 3,000 kilometres an hour.

Scan. Freeze frame.

Notes

Chapter One

1. See P. Virilio, *Défense populaire et luttes écologiques*, Paris 1978.
2. Ortega y Gasset, cited on the masthead of the Chilean far-right paper *Orden Nuevo*.
3. Conversations between the Abbé Pierre and Einstein.
4. See P. Virilio, 'L'Evangile nucléaire', in *L'Insécurité du territoire*, Paris 1976.
5. Norman Kagan, *The Cinema of Stanley Kubrick*, New York 1972, p. 140.
6. Speech of 14 January 1981, *Historic Documents of 1981*, Washington, D.C. 1982, p. 34.
7. Veit Harlan, *Le cinéma allemand selon Goebbels*, Paris 1974.
8. Ibid.
9. The fifties saw fresh attempts to create surprise effects: Cinemascope, Cinerama, 3-D, etc.
10. Aldous Huxley, *The Art of Seeing*, London 1943.

Chapter Two

1. Kevin Brownlow, *Hollywood: The Pioneers*, London 1979, p. 63.
2. Ibid., p. 64.
3. 'The Work of Art in the Age of Mechanical Reproduction', in *Illuminations*, London 1973, p. 236.
4. For Benjamin, whereas 'a clock that is working will always be a disturbance on the stage . . ., film can, whenever appropriate, use time as measured by a clock' (ibid., p. 249). Benjamin saw in this a reciprocity of action between object and man that could be placed at the service of materialist thought. Today it seems more like a proof of the independence of cinema time.
5. 'My desire is where I'm firing at.' Guillaume Apollinaire, from 'Désir' in 'Lueurs des Tirs', *Calligrammes*, Paris 1918.
6. Luigi Pirandello, *Shoot! The Notebooks of Serafino Gubbio, Cinematograph Operator*, London 1927, p. 20.
7. Brownlow, op. cit., p. 71.
8. Ibid., p. 71.
9. Interview on French television.
10. Giovanni Lista, *Marinetti*, Paris 1976.

11. In *Les Carabiniers* (1963) Godard draws a parallel between the dive-bomber and the picture postcard. In 1914 Apollinaire's first *calligramme* incorporated a postcard from his brother, and in the same year Marinetti wove into the film texture of *Zang Toumb Toumb* the full text of a leaflet dropped by a Bulgarian aeroplane during the Balkan War. On 9 August 1918 the Italian 'Serenissimo' squadron, under d'Annunzio's command, saturated Vienna with leaflets. After the 1870–71 war, the postcard industry launched the transporting of photography with cheap, *mediated*, often anonymous images for a mass market. Apart from their sentimental, erotic or merely product-boosting pictures, these postcards were the bearers of nationalist-revanchist or scientistic propaganda and the promotion of high birth-rates. Above all, many of them prefigured surrealist collage with their photographic assembling of real landscape views, hand-drawn adjuncts, science-fiction vessels and burlesque human shapes. Their aesthetic vision was close to that of Méliès or Zecca in the future world of cinema.

12. Quoted from Allan Sekula, 'The Instrumental Image: Steichen at War', *ArtForum*, December 1975, p. 33.

13. In 1919 Vertov published an article in Mayakovsky's avant-garde *Lef* which condemned the narrative film and, in terms reminiscent of the Futurists, declared war on the psychology of bourgeois film-scripts.

14. See Sekula's absorbing study (op. cit.), which has been extensively used in this account of Steichen's activity.

15. See the special issue of *Cahiers du cinéma*: 'Spécial photos de films', 1978.

16. Interview on French television.

17. One of the first happened to be called *General Custer's Revenge*; in it, a model of the general wearing no more than a cap can be moved around in an ambush-ridden desert. The action ends with the rape of a squaw.

18. Brownlow, op. cit., p. 157.

19. Ibid., p. 157.

20. Kagan, op. cit.

21. See Rudolf Arnheim, *Visual Thinking*, Berkeley 1969, p. 33.

22. Benjamin, op. cit., pp. 235–6.

23. Letter from Gance to Culture Minister Jacques Duhamel, 5 August 1972.

24. Amos Vogel, *Film as a Subversive Art*, London 1974, p. 36. Cf. Gyorgy Kepes, *Language of Vision*, New York 1967.

25. See Erich Mendelsohn, *Das Gesamtschaffen des Architekten*, Berlin 1930.

26. See Lotte Eisner, *L'écran démoniaque*, Paris 1981.

27. Noël Simsolo, 'Le cinéma allemand sous Guillaume II', *La Revue de cinéma*, September 1982.

28. Gustave Le Bon, *Enseignements psychologiques de la guerre européenne*. Paris 1916.

Chapter Three

1. See Francis Lacloche, *Architecture de cinémas*, Paris 1981.

2. The term '*mois du blanc*' is still used in France to refer to the period immediately after Christmas when the big stores replace toys and other seasonal goods in their windows with sale goods (originally towels, tablecloths and other such items which, in the last century, were invariably white).

3. John Locke, *An Essay Concerning Human Understanding*, quoted from Arnheim, op. cit., p. 154.

4. Rothapfel, who was known as 'Roxy', persuaded the owner of the *Alhambra* music-hall in Milwaukee to turn it into a cinema. The idea was an immediate success and Roxy went on to set up the first giant movie-houses in New York (Regent, Rialto, Capitol, etc.). The Roxy cinema itself, which was opened by Gloria Swanson in 1927, cost 12 million dollars and could hold an audience of 6,200. It was pulled down in 1960, 'after a final homage to the star worthy of *Sunset Boulevard*, and accompanied by the sound of mechanical excavators' (Lacloche, op. cit.). Rothapfel, of course, was of German origin, and we should not forget that the Germans had built huge cinemas well before the Americans and

other Europeans. (Many of their Palast houses opened before 1914 and were destroyed by bombing during the Second World War.) The architecture of German thirties cinemas was resolutely 'modern' and drew its inspiration from the Dynamists – the Lichtburg in Berlin, as its name suggests, was a fortress of light, a camera obscura illuminating the city with its powerful beams.

5. Evry Schatzmann, 'La cosmologie: physique nouvelle ou classique?', *La Recherche* No. 91, 1978.

6. Nicole Loraux, 'L'autochtonie athénienne, le mythe dans l'espace civique', *Annales*, January–February 1979.

7. Walter Laquer, *The Terrible Secret: An Investigation into the Suppression of Information about Hitler's 'Final Solution'*, London 1980. Cf. G.H. Rabinovitch, 'Le chêne de Buchenwald', *Traces* No. 3.

8. Goebbels was so excited about the uses of rumour that he wanted to make a film about the subject. Although this project came to nothing, the *Reichsministerium* went on to the very end flooding the press, radio and cinema with heavily massaged news in which photographic 'authenticity' backed up the false reports being put into circulation. The technique dates back a long time, but the Nazis knew how to integrate it perfectly into their military strategy, a good example being the mass exodus that they triggered during the French campaign in 1940.

9. Nicole Loraux, *Les enfants d'Athéna*, Paris 1981.

10. Quoted from Abel Gance's shooting diary.

11. Quoted from the Marey *Monographie*, Ed. Centre Georges Pompidou, Paris 1977.

12. In *La terre et les rêveries de la volonté*, Bachelard notes that the dream may be understood as a sequence of images which may correspond to a sequence in waking life. See Jacques Dournes, *Forêt, Femme, Folie*, Paris 1978; and Jean and Françoise Duvignaud, Jean-Pierre Corbeau, *La banque des rêves*, Paris 1979.

13. Octave Mirbeau, *La 628-E-8*, Paris 1905.

14. Michèle Lagny, Marie-Claire Ropars, Pierre Sorlin, *La révolution figurée*, Paris 1979.

15. Quoted in Brownlow, op. cit., p. 80.

16. Marcel Pagnol, *Confidences*, Paris 1981.

17. Lewis Feuer, 'A Critical Evaluation', in *New Politics*.

18. Interview on French television.

19. *The Diaries of Franz Kafka*, ed. Max Brod, Harmondworth 1964, p. 393.

20. For a discussion of the term 'proxemic', see Edward T. Hall, *The Hidden Dimension*, London 1966, p. 1.

21. During the fighting that often accompanied migration, women's role as male-controlled carriers allowed the hunter to specialize in the homosexual duel – to become, in other words, a killer of men, a warrior. Whereas battles had previously been restricted by the low mobility of ethnic groups, they could now range over wide spaces as women provided rear support and passed up the supply of projectiles. Thanks to the invention of this form of livestock, the male possessed a good capacity for movement, and until the domestication of the horse heterosexual groups were more formidable than homosexual associations. *The female thus twice helped the male to come into the world*: first at birth, and then by making a warrior of him. At once the first means of species transport (in pregnancy and early childhood) and the first form of 'logistical support', women laid the basis for war by freeing the hunter of the need to assure his own maintenance. This explains why the Greek military dream, for example – with its focus on Athena – went far beyond the masculine–feminine opposition or the sexual non-realism of the nineteenth and twentieth centuries.

22. See the material edited by Janet Finkelstein for the *Cahiers d'Etudes stratégiques* No. 1.

Chapter Four

1. P. Virilio, *Vitesse et politique*, Paris 1977.

2. Ernst Jünger, *In Stahlgewittern* (translated here from the French edition, *Orages*

d'acier, Paris 1970).

3. In *Cahiers du cinéma* (No. 311), Samuel Fuller argued that it was impossible to film the Normandy landing because you couldn't decently film yards of intestine on a beach. Apart from the fact that dead people do not take well to being photographed (see the pictures of assassinations or traffic accidents), Fuller's witticism suggests that military–industrial films cannot *decently* be horror films, since in one way or another they are intended to embellish death. Moreover, the Allied landing acutely re-posed the problem of documentary realism. Today everyone knows that there were not yards of intestine on the Normandy beaches and that the landing was a remarkable and technically difficult operation – not because of German resistance (which was virtually non-existent), but because of the adverse weather and the complicated Normandy countryside. Thus, *in order to make up the numbers*, the Allied commanders threw their men into operations like the storming of Hoc Point, which were as suicidal as they were spectacular. In 1962, when Zanuck made his fictional documentary with fifty stars, 20,000 extras and six directors, the action took place on the Ile de Ré or in Spain, where the beaches were 'grander' than those of Arromanche. This immortalization of a battle that had never happened ensured that *The Longest Day* was a great box-office success.

4. P. Virilio, *Bunker archéologie*, Paris 1975.

Chapter Five

1. Brownlow, *Hollywood*, op. cit., p. 80.
2. Ibid., p. 81.
3. On Rosavita, see Gillo Dorflès, *Le kitsch*, Paris 1978.
4. Testimony of Rudolf Hess: Speer, *Journal de Spandau*, p. 401. Fern Andra, an Austrian like Hitler, had been a popular actress in silent films. The cinema had changed its name to the Atrium.
5. Arnheim points out, however, that the abstract design of the swastika drew heavily upon a powerful 'explanatory context'. He recalls that when Hitler made a visit to Mussolini, Rome was covered overnight with swastikas and an Italian girl exclaimed in horror: 'Rome is crawling with black spiders.' *Visual Thinking*, op. cit., pp. 143–44.
6. Vogel, op. cit., p. 176.
7. *Signal*, 1941. This magazine was the French edition of *Berliner Illustrierte Zeitung*, which appeared in most European languages including English.
8. See Anthony Cave Brown, *Bodyguard of Lies*, London 1976.
9. The highly dream-like quality of Harlan's remembrances makes them an irreplaceable testimony on *cinema according to Goebbels*.
10. Quoted in J. MacGovern, *Crossbow and Overcast*, London 1965, p. 21.
11. In a memorandum of 28 August 1945, President Truman ordered the concealment from the public of all information relating to the techniques, methods and results, both past and present, of any code-breaking department. The Allies had a number of good reasons for acting in this way, particularly the fear that a war with the Russians would require *Ultra* and so on to come back into service.

Chapter Six

1. In January 1940 the British Ministry of Information published a memorandum on the state of the army's photography and film departments. In fact it wished to carry out a revolution by halting distribution of military documentaries that were considered too static and technical and therefore incapable of assisting the unprecedented war effort. The great photographer Cecil Beaton was to play a dominant role in implementing this reform. We should remember that in response to the nationalization of the Soviet cinema, an effective documentary school had been founded in 1928 with the support of men like Rudyard Kipling, the senior civil servant Stephen Tallents, and the film-maker John Grierson. This movement, which was conceived as a public service and enjoyed state subsidies, made a

considerable international impact. It also led indirectly to the formation of the Crown Film Unit, the largest producer of British propaganda films during the war, which was based in the requisitioned Pinewood Studios. Cavalcanti was its director until 1940.

2. Ian Goodhope Colvin, *Flight 777*, London 1957, pp. 48–49.

3. Cave Brown, *Bodyguard of Lies*, p. 603.

4. Paul Scanlon and Michael Gross, *The Book of Alien*, London 1979, unpaginated.

5. Quoted from 'Made in USA', *Cahiers du cinéma*, April 1982.

6. Ibid.

7. Andrew Stratton, in Nigel Calder, ed., *Unless Peace Come*, Harmondsworth 1968, p. 98.

Chapter Seven

1. To a large extent naval battles had long anticipated this type of practice.

2. Antoine de St-Exupéry, *Pilote de Guerre*, Paris 1981.

3. A. Speer, *Au coeur du Troisième Reich* and *Le journal de Spandau*.

4. For the Americans, the abstractness of their recapture of the Pacific islands made 'cinema direction' a necessity – hence the importance of the camera crews committed to the campaign.

5. The *commissaire aux montres* was the officer responsible for inspecting weapons and equipment under the Ancien Régime.

6. 'It's raining my soul, it's raining, but it's raining dead eyes.' Guillaume Apollinaire, from 'La nuit d'avril 1915' in 'Case d'Armons', *Calligrammes*, Paris 1918.

7. See the report of the seminar '*Le cinéma grande vitesse* – instrumentations et applications', ANRT, Paris, December 1981.

8. Colonel Jack Broughton, *Thud Ridge*, Philadelphia and New York 1969, p. 110.

9. Ibid., pp. 92–93.

10. Ibid., p. 98.